THE
RULE
OF
ONE

ADVANCE PRAISE FOR THE BOOK

'The authors provide an engaging narrative of their incredible experiential learning as they went on to demonstrate the power of social intrapreneurship. Their shared learnings have led to an invaluable guidebook that is fascinating and very timely! A must-read.'

R.A. MASHELKAR,
Padma Vibushan;
national research professor;
former director general, CSIR;
president, Indian National Science Academy;
chairman, National Innovation Foundation

'We need to find ways to create opportunities for people to unleash their unlimited creative powers to overcome the barriers imposed by our flawed economic thinking. This book provides an example for aspiring entrepreneurs of a social business that uses technology to do just that.'

MUHAMMAD YUNUS,
Noble Peace Prize winner and
author of *The World of Three Zeros*

'This book is an essential guide for anyone interested in how a modern corporation used intrapreneurship and social innovation to affect lasting change for people in impoverished areas of the world. Students and professionals alike will be inspired by what can be accomplished when new approaches are embraced.'

SANDRA MORRIS,
former CIO, Intel Corporation

KAZI I. HUQUE

NARAYAN SUNDARARAJAN

JACEN GREENE

THE RULE OF ONE

The Power of

SOCIAL

INTRAPRENEURSHIP

PORTFOLIO
PENGUIN

An imprint of Penguin Random House

PORTFOLIO

USA | Canada | UK | Ireland | Australia
New Zealand | India | South Africa | China

Portfolio is part of the Penguin Random House group of companies
whose addresses can be found at global.penguinrandomhouse.com

Published by Penguin Random House India Pvt. Ltd
7th Floor, Infinity Tower C, DLF Cyber City,
Gurgaon 122 002, Haryana, India

Penguin
Random House
India

First published in Portfolio by Penguin Random House India 2019

ISBN 9780670092376

Typeset in Sabon by Manipal Digital Systems, Manipal
Printed at Thomson Press India Ltd, New Delhi

www.penguin.co.in

MIX
Paper
FSC FSC® C010615

CONTENTS

FOREWORD

Technology will keep on changing the world. There is nothing new about it. It has been happening since human beings have inhabited this planet. Technology is changing faster and faster. Where it took a century for change to happen, it takes a decade now. Soon it will be done in a day or less. But the big question is: What direction will this change be directed at? It can create a world of three zeros—zero poverty, zero unemployment, zero net carbon emission—any time it wants. But are we directing the technology that way. Technology has the power to take us anywhere we want to go. But where do we want to go? Have we decided that?

When I founded Grameen Bank, I wanted to find a way to provide credit to those who needed it the most, but were turned away by the traditional banks. Through our work over the years, we have established the fact that it can be done in a financially sustainable way anywhere in the world. Again the question is: Are we willing to do it? It is no longer a question of whether it can be done.

Utilizing information technology and having it play a bigger role in addressing poverty was a key and an important next step, and former Intel CEO Craig Barrett and I saw an opportunity to bring technology to other fields which do not get much attention from the technology world. In doing so I soon met Kazi Huque and, later, Narayan Sundararajan, from Intel USA. They saw the possibilities to use the power of technology to ensure that people at the bottom have the same access to information technology as those at the top. Over the years, they became true entrepreneurs within a large corporation. Grameen Intel got started on a small scale with the same energy as a Silicon Valley start-up. The venture continues to inspire the creation of new gadgets, new software and, one day, hopefully, new chips.

This is a practitioner's guide that shares some of the lessons they learned along the way. Forming a social business was only the beginning. Both Kazi and Narayan, along with Jacen Greene, touch upon the challenges they faced and the ways they went about tackling those. They outline how they brought business, technology and research expertise to address a host of issues in healthcare, education and agriculture.

Through the various chapters, the reader will benefit from learning ground-level realities. The authors have shared their experiences very candidly. They have covered areas where they have been successful, as well as what they would have done differently. The creative approach they outlined in the book can be used by any foundation, social business and development agency.

I hope more individuals will step up to become social business entrepreneurs, intrapreneurs in a large corporation, or part of a social business start-up. Individually or as part of a corporation interested in playing a direct role in changing the world, we can overcome many of the problems faced by society today. What is needed is a dedicated and focused effort towards those goals through a business format which doesn't distract it by imposing the mission of making profits for the shareholders of the company.

Professor Muhammad Yunus
Founder of Grameen Bank
Nobel Peace Prize Laureate, 2006

INTRODUCTION

Take out a world map and a pencil. Draw a circle with the centre in Bangladesh and a radius of 1500 miles. The circle covers much of India, Pakistan, China and Indonesia, some of the most densely populated countries in the world. There are more people living inside this circle than outside it, and many of them live in poverty (Quah, 2016).

When people think of economic development in developing countries, they often think of handouts: direct charity, development aid and low-cost loans provided to local governments. However, at the end of the day, the real solution to poverty is economic opportunity through education and jobs. We have seen information technology become a key economic driver in the West. We have seen outsourcing add millions of jobs in India. We have seen banks and microcredit institutions evolve to provide access to credit for the poor. Can we do more to create viable economic solutions using information technology for the impoverished parts of the world?

Efforts in this area thus far have centred on cheap devices, such as a $100 computer and greater broadband internet access, sometimes coupled with additional services. A typical approach is to donate computers to schools and hospitals, or to set up an Internet-enabled service centre in a remote village. The service centre comes with a promise to serve the low-income community by providing, for example, harvest information, or by processing online forms for land registries that help establish ownership claims. These efforts have only generated limited success in alleviating poverty, because more is needed than just setting up a computer with an internet connection. Entire government bureaucracies and organizations have to be created or redesigned to process this information to produce the required output. But more importantly, there has to be clear cash flow for the beneficiary—better agricultural information leads to more income, or the ability to process a land registry leads to lower costs. Our approach to information technology adoption is ineffectual without those clear economic benefits.

In 2007, Craig Barrett was the chairman of Intel Corporation. He had previously served as CEO, and in his new role he acted as a technology ambassador travelling the world. In each country he visited, he met with the leaders of the government and major corporations. He talked about the impact of technology on education and healthcare, and he talked about how countries can catalyse their economic growth through the increased adoption of technology. On one of these trips, he met Muhammad Yunus, who had recently received the Nobel

Peace Prize for his work on microcredit. Yunus shared the prize with Grameen Bank, which he had established to loan small amounts of money to those in poverty for income-generating purposes, enabling millions of people to alleviate their poverty by establishing access to financial credit.

One of the ideas that came up during their discussion was to create a company to focus on how technology solutions might be designed for low-income populations. Could we create solutions and services that had real tangible benefits? Not for the rich, but for the poor— those who were yet to benefit from the incredible growth of information technology. The company would be set up as a social business, a non-loss and non-dividend company. In other words, the company would try to recover its operational costs, but if it generated any surplus cash, that would be reinvested into the company to support its mission.

Intel found two employees, Kazi I. Huque and Narayan Sundararajan, who were passionate about and committed to the use of technology for social impact. We, at different points in our Intel tenure, had pitched other business ideas for how to do that, and this was a perfect opportunity. Setting up a business with a goal for social impact is why we are called social entrepreneurs. When that happens within an existing organization, we refer to ourselves as 'social intrapreneurs'. Here we would be getting a business off the ground with, no doubt, some rather idealistic goals.

We started Grameen Intel with a core focus on information technology as a source of livelihood and income generation, as opposed to the pure consumption of information. At the same time, we wanted to have a positive social impact through better health outcomes, increased agricultural yields and other approaches. Along the way, we realized that solutions tend to become more complicated than the users' requirements, and that economic benefits, such as higher incomes or lower costs, are not always part of the solution design or delivery from the start.

We tackled the first problem, of solutions tending to be more complicated than they need to be, by using Human-Centred Design, through immersion in the lives of those we hoped to benefit. We addressed the second problem—how the solution provides an economic benefit—by understanding their needs and aptitudes so that we could provide an avenue for clear financial benefits to them. This was as much about the technology design as it was about cost-benefit analysis tied to a particular solution. It went back to our key focus areas around economic development: education and jobs, in our case, enabled by information technology. Whatever we created needed to be part of our users' day-to-day lives and their economic reality.

When we analysed the data, we found that nearly half of those living in developing countries have yet to benefit from information technology (Poushter, 2016). For many, this is the frothy economics of the 'next billion' consumers. Instead, what we learnt is that success demands a clear lens on the needs and lifestyles of the people in emerging markets, a laser-sharp focus on products and the stamina to build a model for lasting social and economic impact. It is not about dreaming up new design concepts and marketing them to hit sales targets. It also cannot be what we think they 'need' or is 'good for them', but what they want and are willing to purchase or use. Starting with that in mind, we wanted to share our humble beginnings as social intrapreneurs, and what we learnt along the way, with those who are already on the path or want to join a similar journey.

In Chapter 1, we talk about Kazi's childhood, and how that shaped his interest in social entrepreneurship. We discuss social entrepreneurship as a field and explain why understanding the monetary value of time, irrespective of income, is fundamental to economic and social development. Helping realize that is a long-term goal of Grameen Intel.

Chapter 2 reviews social intrapreneurship—thinking like an entrepreneur for social benefit, but within an existing organization—and how Muhammad Yunus used that approach to launch a host of new social businesses following the success of Grameen Bank. Grameen Intel was one of these social businesses, formed as a partnership between Grameen and Intel, but that creation process was far from easy. However, this process can be made easier for future intrapreneurs by learning from organizations like ours and by following an emerging set of best practices and frameworks.

In Chapter 3, we cover Narayan's childhood in India and his recent encounter with tuberculosis that helped shape his commitment to social impact. We also discuss Grameen Intel's early attempts to understand customer needs using Human-Centred Design, and how we sought to develop healthcare services using the United Nations Millennium Development Goals as a framework.

Chapter 4 discusses the Lean Start-up methodology and Business Model Canvas, and how Grameen Intel employed them to create a successful soil-testing application and a working business model. Prototyping, iterating, learning from our customers, and from our mistakes, enabled a quick pivot from early missteps to laying the foundation for a long-term success.

From soil testing to prenatal healthcare, Chapter 5 details our struggles to create and deploy a new solution in Bangladesh's healthcare system, and how a focus on narrowing the solution through ethnographic research helped bring insight.

Chapter 6 talks about the complexity of reaching a simple design, and how design fundamentals helped expand Grameen Intel's product portfolio into early literacy apps for the education market and wearable air-quality monitors that doubled as jewellery.

Chapter 7 addresses how persistently high global unemployment and underemployment rates demonstrate the importance of developing solutions that enable customers to save money or generate revenue, empowering them as entrepreneurs. At the same time, business modelling and effective marketing are shown to be just as important for social intrapreneurs.

Creating a product that customers want, that generates positive impact, and building a successful business model around it isn't enough. Capital for start-up and growth is also essential. Chapter 8 goes over the capitalization strategy of Grameen Intel and the broader movement of impact investing in support of measurable, intentional, social and environmental impact.

Chapter 9 talks about how you know that you're doing good, not just doing well: the theory and practice of impact measurement and reporting, including logic models, theories of change and clear measurement plans. These approaches are linked to the United Nations Sustainable Development Goals, a global agreement on priorities for positive impact that replaced the Millennium Development Goals.

Chapter 10 addresses the differences between business growth and scaling impact, frameworks for expanding a social business and the challenges of expanding on a global scale. We also walk through Grameen Intel's immediate goals and long-term strategy.

Everyone can be an entrepreneur, and Chapter 11 shows how, with career tips for social intrapreneurs, an overview of the challenges and benefits of social intrapreneurship and some critical lessons learnt.

Every entrepreneur or intrapreneur is also, always, a student or educator of some kind. That's why we include an Educator's Guide for teachers, professors and consultants, with a detailed, chapter-by-chapter breakdown of relevant topics, additional reading, discussion questions and supplementary resources.

ONE

Time Is More than Money

When Kazi I. Huque was growing up in Dhaka, Bangladesh in the 1970s, his grandfather would often take him for a drive. The licence plate on the car was simply the first letter in the Bengali alphabet followed by the number 62—one of the first cars registered in the country. It would take them less than thirty minutes to run out of paved road, in the nation's capital.

Kazi's grandfather, born in what was then British India in 1909, was one of the few who held a coveted government job in the colony. His income ensured a middle-class life for his family throughout the tumultuous period of independence from the British Empire, partition from India, and the later war for independence from Pakistan. British India, East Pakistan, Bangladesh: three different names for the same region in less than thirty years. Migration, warfare and famine destabilized the country and led to images of poverty that flashed by

the car's window as Kazi drove through Dhaka with his
grandfather.

Twenty years later, after completing his education
and immigrating to the United States, Kazi was in Dhaka
to help establish Grameen Intel Social Business. The
joint economic and social imperatives of the company
followed, in a way, the entrepreneurial examples set by
his parents. Kazi's father was a founding member of the
Bangladesh office of a large multinational accounting
firm, and his mother was instrumental in establishing
the first special education school in the country.

Back in the country of his birth, Kazi's commute to
the Grameen Intel office was nearly the same as those
early drives with his grandfather. There were more lanes,
but the roads were the same length, and a drive that used
to take half an hour now took two. In twenty years,
the population of Bangladesh increased by fifty per cent
to nearly 160 million—a number half of that of the
United States in a country roughly the size of Wisconsin.
Traffic had grown commensurately, with cars bumper-
to-bumper and pedestrians, buses, trucks, rickshaws,
bicycles and motorbikes jostling for space. Kazi had seen
ambulances with their sirens blaring sitting stationary in
traffic, no other vehicle moving to give way.

Like the commute, the faces outside have changed
little as well, except in number. There were the homeless
asking for money. There were those who came to the
capital looking for opportunities. Those who were simply
rushing to work: office workers, day labourers and
construction workers. Middle-class children in uniform
on their way to school. All in the midst of traffic jam,

a chaos representative of the economic forces affecting the poor in many developing nations. They have few options; stuck in a situation they could not control, at the mercy of poor planning and infrastructure. What was their ladder for economic progress?

Many are familiar with the 'time value of money'—if you receive $100 now, it's worth more than receiving it five years in the future, because you can invest it now and receive interest, and because the purchasing power will be stronger now than after five years of inflation. As a finance professional at Intel, this is at the core of what Kazi did for various investment options. But we pay little attention to the value of time when we think about the poor. What is the *monetary* value of their time?

When we talk about the economic benefits that a technology solution will bring, the math needs to be a part of the solution. The source of this realization came from Kazi's observation that the poor were actually incurring higher costs due to inefficiencies in their day-to-day lives, and that idle time was preventing them from realizing income-generating opportunities.

Looking at the economic harm caused simply by traffic jams provides a window into the cost of inefficiency and poorly designed systems. If Kazi spent four hours a day commuting—more than fifteen per cent of his entire day—that means if he had remained in Dhaka and spent fifty years in the workforce, he could expect to spend 7.5 years sitting in traffic. What else could he be doing with that time? What are the macro-level economic effects, the blow to productivity and GDP of millions of people spending years of their lives in traffic?

Let's do a simple math problem using an average life expectancy in the United States of eighty years, and further assuming that most people will work from the ages of twenty-two to sixty-five. In those forty-three years, let's assume an average income of $55,000 per year, which is $2,365,000 through your working life. If you were idle 7.5 years or seventeen per cent of it, that is $412,500 of lost income. That is the money-value-of-time for those idle years.

For most of us reading this book, that number is striking, but for those living on a per capita income of $1,200 per year, that impact of idle time is even more devastating if you were to do a similar money-value-of-time calculation. Most of the workers in this part of the world are not salaried employees but daily wage earners who are incurring a real loss of income. How many more rides could a rickshaw driver have taken during that idle time? What is the number of unpaid hours for a bricklayer? That also means, there is a higher cost to everything: day-to-day essentials cost more from the increased transportation time and chance of spoilage, and services are more expensive or less accessible due to the decreased availability of teachers, healthcare workers and other commuters. And for the person in that stopped ambulance, traffic may be the difference between life and death.

We can extrapolate the lost time and productivity from that traffic to other similarly neglected systems: power, water and sewerage; Internet connectivity and phone lines; shipping and inventory management; healthcare, education and government services. Poor planning, poor infrastructure and lack of timely, accurate and actionable information cause real harm, not just inconvenience, in countries where large segments live in poverty. For them, a few hours of lost productivity can mean the difference between earning enough to eat and going hungry.

In the United States, we try to avoid inefficiencies in various ways so that it actually costs less for the ultimate consumer. For example, Walmart manages inventory using sophisticated computer modelling and just-in-time delivery, reducing the ultimate costs that middle-class families in the US have to pay for their purchases. Mobile banking apps allow you to bank remotely so you don't need to spend time and money walking into a bank.

Efficiency is not just for convenience. It can be a powerful tool to alleviate poverty and reduce suffering, if employed well with a goal to provide economic benefits. But, at the root of those efficient systems is a society built on universal access to quality education, infrastructure that enables the free flow of goods, people and information, and the technology to coordinate it all. For Kazi, that was the starting point. He was fortunate enough to receive a good education, to secure a job at a large technology company in the US, and to move to a country with good infrastructure. The country he grew up in could offer only a few of those things. How, he wondered, could he bridge the two and make a difference in the world?

When Grameen Intel was formed in 2009, the question of how to effectively deploy solutions in healthcare, education, agriculture and other sectors in developing nations was hotly contested. Existing models for international aid and development had been under heavy criticism for years. The dominant twentieth-century paradigm of global, top-down aid initiatives led by governments and development agencies was criticized for its apparent ineffectiveness, lack of transparency, inclusiveness or accountability, and approaches that often seemed designed to create political or market benefits for donor countries.

Meanwhile, the 'appropriate technology' movement was opposed by entrepreneurs like Martin Fisher, co-founder and CEO of non-profit KickStart, for favouring expensive or ineffective solutions, designed by outsiders, that ignored local needs and failed to utilize economic incentives or market systems. After working directly with, and then abandoning the appropriate technology movement, KickStart was designed

> to use a market-based model in which we would sell our new technologies directly to local entrepreneurs. We would identify profitable business models that thousands of people could start; design the tools and equipment needed to make these businesses possible; and most importantly, establish a private-sector supply chain to manufacture, distribute, and sell the new tools and equipment to the entrepreneurs (Fisher, 2006).

This 'social enterprise' approach enabled KickStart to help 170,000 families start their own businesses using their products between 1991 and 2014 (KickStart, 2017).

Muhammad Yunus, founder of Grameen Bank, co-recipient of the 2006 Nobel Peace Prize, had introduced a similar model to the world of finance. Yunus had left Bangladesh to study, and later teach, economics in the United States, but returned after his home country's war for independence. While working to improve agricultural yields in villages suffering from the terrible famine that followed the war, Yunus realized that access to formal credit was virtually non-existent. Instead, poor farmers turned to usurious moneylenders for the cash they needed to purchase essential seeds, fertilizer and tools. The extremely high interest rates charged on such loans often led to default, requiring poor villagers to take out another loan from the moneylender to pay the first, and accelerating a cycle of worsening indebtedness and poverty (Yunus, 2008).

In a famous experiment, Yunus lent $27 of his own money to forty-two poor villagers, enough to help them repay their loans from moneylenders. Seeking a more permanent solution, Yunus approached traditional banks in Bangladesh that had previously refused to serve the poor because they lacked collateral. He offered to serve as guarantor, and started a lending programme that achieved a nearly 100 per cent repayment rate. Heartened by the success of the programme, and convinced that access to credit was a 'fundamental human right', Yunus started his own bank: Grameen, which means 'village' in Bangla (Yunus, 2008).

The microfinance model spread in Bangladesh by Grameen Bank helped those most in need establish credit, repay informal loans and launch income-generating businesses. Lending to small groups and establishing education, disbursement and repayment centres in local villages, Grameen Bank was able to ensure a nearly ninety-eight per cent repayment rate. Between late 1970s and 2014, Grameen Bank lent nearly $16 billion (Grameen Communications, 2014). Buoyed by the success of their model, Grameen established a trust to launch partnerships and ventures in other sectors. In 2007, Intel Chairman Craig Barrett and Muhammad Yunus talked about a possible joint collaboration, the concept that would become the Grameen Intel company.

In 2009, the same year that Grameen Intel was launched, Daniel Kaufmann of the Brookings Institution lamented that 'path-breaking IT innovations' and 'market- and private-driven solutions to development challenges' were almost completely absent from high-level talks on aid, despite their demonstrated effectiveness (Kaufmann, 2009). Grameen Intel would seek to fill that gap, using Grameen's proven grass-roots design and distribution approaches to adapt and utilize Intel technologies, previously designed only for the world's richest twenty per cent to meet the pressing needs of the global poor.

The new company would seek to use information technology products and services to alleviate poverty through income-generating methods. In response to the successes, and failures, of previous approaches, and motivated by Kazi and Narayan's commitment to setting up a company with a social mission, a market-based solution and a proven model from Grameen were two key pillars that they took note of. In addition, incorporating the monetary value of time was their first rule (of eleven) to guide their model.

In this way, by pursuing the new social enterprise model of development, they hoped to address the poverty-related issues they had seen when they were growing up and fulfil their commitment to creating a better world.

TWO

Think Like an Entrepreneur Inside Your Organization

High-tech companies have to keep the engine of innovation alive to remain competitive, and many companies have transformed themselves to enter new lines of business to grow or simply stay alive. In 1985, Intel became a microprocessor company when faced with growing competition from Japan in the memory business. Andy Grove, their outspoken CEO, coined the phrase 'only the paranoid survive'.

That spirit is alive at Intel. There are nascent businesses that include programmable chips, artificial intelligence, and a few hundred other product ideas. These are run by entrepreneurs who are tasked to grow the business. Not all of them succeed, and when that happens their resources are reallocated to the next big idea. Another way to maintain competitiveness is through investing in or acquiring external companies which have developed innovative new products or services. Intel created an investment division, Intel Capital, to do this. Grameen Intel bridged Intel's world of corporate entrepreneurship and investment when it received seed money from Intel Capital, providing Kazi and his team the opportunity to be true 'intrapreneurs'.

In 1978, Gifford Pinchot III coined the term 'intrapreneur' to describe someone exhibiting entrepreneurial behaviour within an existing organization:

> *We have two problems which are really one. The first is how to grant idea people the independence they desire without making them unresponsive to the needs of the corporation. The second is how to make the corporation more capable of responding rapidly and sensitively to our rapidly changing society. These problems can be resolved by setting up a system allowing selected employees a status within the corporation akin to that of the entrepreneur within the larger society. This new status must provide them with the independence of the entrepreneur while still holding over them the technological, financial, and perhaps most significant, the informational umbrella of the corporation.*

The corporate intrapreneur would take on some of the risks of designing and launching a new venture from within the organization, including internal or external fundraising, but would receive greater freedom to shape their role and concept. In doing so, the corporation would 'allow people to lead lives which more fully express their potential' (Pinchot, 1978). Muhammad Yunus would take the concept even further, embracing intrapreneurship as a model that enabled not only the intrapreneur but also their customers and beneficiaries to achieve their greatest potential.

Following the success of Grameen Bank, Grameen Trust was established in 1989 to scale the Grameen model through technical assistance and capacity building for other microfinance institutions worldwide. It also aimed to support the establishment of 'social businesses' through joint ventures and direct investments. Yunus used the term to describe a financially sustainable company that was dedicated to addressing a social problem through provision of a beneficial product or service, 'Type I', or that was directly owned by the poor and provided them clear financial returns, 'Type II'. Unlike a Type II social business, Type I could not pay out dividends; instead, profits were reinvested in growing the business and its benefits. Investors could therefore recover only their initial investment, but not earn a return (Yunus, 2010).

'Whenever I wanted to deal with a social or economic problem, I tried to solve the problem by creating a business around it,' said Yunus (2010). Among the many businesses Grameen launched were:

- Grameen Phone, a joint venture with Telenor Group, which by 2010 was the largest tax-paying company in Bangladesh, and by 2014 the largest telecom provider in the country with more than fifty million subscribers. Its Village Phone

Program helped more than 200,000 'phone ladies' purchase a cell phone with a loan from Grameen Bank and sell calls to their neighbours, turning them into micro-entrepreneurs (Grameenphone).

- Grameen Shakti, which sold solar home installations, biogas plants, and cooking stoves through credit and established a network of small-scale manufacturers and entrepreneurs to support the model. Through 2013, Grameen Shakti had installed solar systems on 1.3 million homes, many of which had no access to an existing electrical grid (Grameen Shakti).

- Grameen Healthcare Trust, which provided micro insurance offerings, operated forty-eight small clinics, and managed an eye hospital (Grameen Healthcare Trust). Grameen Danone, a joint venture between the eponymous organizations that sold children's yogurt fortified with micronutrients, and Grameen Veolia, another joint venture that provided clean drinking water, were related efforts focused on health.

By creating organizations with distinct structures, approaches, and funding, each of these new social businesses could pursue their preferred approach to addressing their targeted problems without having to fit within an existing Grameen model. This was the case with Grameen Intel, an idea sparked by a conversation between Muhammad Yunus and Intel Corporation's Chairman of the Board and former CEO, Craig Barrett. In 2007, Barrett was in Bangladesh on behalf of Intel's World Ahead Programme, an initiative to expand information technology access at the base of the pyramid. At that time, Barrett was also chair of the United Nations Global Alliance for ICT (Information and Communications Technology) and Development, testament to his interest in finding technology solutions to poverty.

At the World Ahead meeting, Yunus met Barrett, described his concept for a social business, and discussed potential ideas for a joint venture between Grameen and Intel. A working group of managers from both organizations was formed to develop a concept for the proposed venture, and they narrowed in on a concept that they believed would successfully link Intel's technology expertise with Grameen's grass-roots approach to social impact.

As Barrett described it on his company blog in 2008:

> *The business model is remarkably similar to the Grameen 'phone ladies:' Financing will be provided at the local level to allow individuals to buy computers, printers and Internet access. These individuals can then act as a village resource to sell services that would not otherwise be available. Initially services such as telemedicine, simple financial transactions, education and training and others are envisioned. The service business will be entrepreneurial, sustainable, and a benefit to the local community (Yunus, 2014).*

At that time, Kazi Huque had recently completed his MBA and was working as a finance manager for the software division. He wasn't yet involved with the Grameen Intel concept, although, he had followed Grameen Bank for years and had even once helped Muhammad Yunus with another information technology project. When Kazi was in high school, the accounting firm that his father worked for was Grameen Bank's first auditor. In 1984, Grameen Bank had received a donation of two computers from USAID, but nobody at the organization had worked with a computer before. Kazi, who had become a bit of a computer prodigy after playing with a Texas Instruments TI-99/4A his father brought home after a trip from England—even going so far as to train his father's accounting colleagues in spreadsheet software—set up the new computers for Grameen Bank and met Yunus afterwards. Twenty-four years later, Kazi would run into Yunus again, now a Nobel Laureate and global celebrity, at a 2008 book signing in Portland, Oregon.

After the event, Kazi reintroduced himself to Yunus, and they chatted briefly. Yunus asked where he worked, and when Kazi mentioned Intel, Yunus suggested that he talk to Craig Barrett about the Grameen Intel concept. Although Kazi was interested, he didn't expect a reply from Intel's chairman, and so he emailed several managers involved with the project, to little effect. Finally, in frustration, he sent a late-night email directly to Barrett's company account.

At that moment, Barrett was in Davos attending the World Economic Forum. Kazi received a reply 'in less than five minutes' directing him to the company's chief legal counsel and head of Corporate Social Responsibility

(CSR), who was hiring a team for Grameen Intel. Another email and thirty minutes later, Kazi was informally connected to the project—but it wasn't going anywhere. For nearly six months, there was little traction and no official role for Kazi. Then, finally, the vice president of Intel Capital for Asia called up Kazi and asked him to meet with Yunus as a replacement for an existing team member.

Intel Capital, which had been working on the proposed concept, was a natural partner for Grameen Trust. Formed in 1991 as an internal private equity fund with the goal of 'building technology ecosystems', Intel Capital was a perfect complement to Grameen Trust's model of expanding microfinance worldwide. Within fifteen years of its inception, the fund had invested roughly USD $11.4 billion in more than 1,400 companies. The fund's impressive track record included 570 exits by investees, either through issuing an Initial Public Offering on a stock market, merging with another company, or by an acquisition in a purchase agreement (Intel Capital).

Intel Capital was willing to forgo their usual returns if they invested in a new company formed in partnership with Grameen, but they needed a clear plan for the business, and Barrett wanted to see a model that would open up the vast market in developing nations to Intel products. However, Yunus didn't have the deep expertise in technology needed to propose a specific model, and Intel Capital was focused on using the partnership as a way to further the World Ahead agenda. World Ahead was committed to vastly expanded global internet connectivity and information flow offered through thousands of village internet kiosks, something that Yunus felt wouldn't sufficiently address the pressing and immediate needs of the 'extremely poor'. Kazi's role in Bangladesh was to get the partnership back on track and to come up with a working model for Grameen Intel.

Kazi arrived in Dhaka (at a Grameen building that was much larger than that of his last visit) to find that Grameen had booked a room for Intel's 'delegation', which consisted only of him and the head of Intel's Bangladesh office. Kazi prepared a three-slide proposal for Yunus, focused on providing healthcare information services and other products that would enable users to act as entrepreneurs, offering the service for a small fee. He believed that, 'You can't just sell information. Nobody's interested in your advice. It has to be an income opportunity.' The slides and language used in the presentation were based on Kazi's research into how Yunus preferred to communicate. The plan itself was based on Kazi's perception of the need in Bangladesh and was a major departure from the previous discussions. By coincidence, Yunus brought a magazine article into the meeting on Craig Barrett's work in telemedicine. Although the meeting was scheduled for an hour, it lasted only forty minutes. At the end, Yunus said simply, 'Let's start work.'

On his return in July 2008, Kazi briefed Intel Capital on the meeting. He had operated with the 'independence of an entrepreneur', and now needed to determine if he had the 'technological, financial, and informational umbrella of the corporation' overhead to support his initiative. After the briefing, he was placed in charge of the project. He had two years to develop the model, create a business plan, and secure start-up funding, a familiar role for a software entrepreneur, but a radical change for a financial manager.

Luckily, the head of finance at Intel Capital offered him a position after his time at Grameen Intel expired. With a backup plan in hand, Kazi felt comfortable jumping into his new role as a social intrapreneur. However, the proposed venture would still need to meet not only the demands of any new business but also the unique requirements and pathway of an intrapreneurial endeavour.

Kazi at this point had the start of a business concept, but he needed a technology expert. This person, though, also had to understand the needs of low-income customers, be aware of local ecosystem and the issues in south Asia, and have a personal commitment to creating positive social impact. He found this person in Narayan Sundararajan, who was introduced to him through a Bangladeshi-born Intel engineer working in California. Narayan was then working in the emerging markets healthcare division at Intel, but he had a broader passion for using technology for driving social impact.

Perhaps unknowingly, Kazi and Narayan were not only acting like intrapreneurs but also following the stages of intrapreneurship as identified by Alistair Croll and Ben Yoskovitz (2013) as essential for success. The six key stages are discussed here:

1. Beforehand: establish buy-in and understand success metrics
2. Empathy: develop a clear understanding of the customer problem
3. Stickiness: create a 'minimum viable product' or service to test demand
4. Virality: enable customers to easily share their product/service experience with others
5. Revenue: understand how to generate revenue within your organization's existing model, channels, and agreements
6. Scale: embed the new venture within the existing organization to ensure longevity and growth

At the first stage, Croll and Yoskovitz argue that intrapreneurs need executive buy-in, a clear understanding of the metrics by which they will be judged, the rules they must follow, and the resources they will be able to use. However, this sidelines some of the very things that make an intrapreneur that person with 'the independence of the entrepreneur' different from a traditional manager. The savvy intrapreneur, one who truly embodies the fundamental tenets of entrepreneurship, might negotiate the metrics, obtain prior approval to break certain rules, and work to secure additional internal or external resources for their venture.

These are some of the behaviours that J. Gregory Dees identified in his definitive definition of 'social entrepreneurs' as individuals who:

play the role of change agents in the social sector, by:
adopting a mission to create and sustain social value
(not just private value); recognizing and relentlessly
pursuing new opportunities to serve that mission;
engaging in a process of continuous innovation,
adaptation, and learning; acting boldly without
being limited by resources currently in hand; and
exhibiting a heightened sense of accountability to the
constituencies served and for the outcomes created
(Dees, 2001).

Acting without regard to the limitations of currently
available resources (which Dees described as the factor
that most often circumscribes a typical manager's role) is
fundamental to the social entrepreneur, and, therefore,
to the social intrapreneur. Indeed, as Kazi led Grameen
Intel through the earliest stages of its development, he
worked to define the success metrics in dialogue with
Intel and Grameen leadership, pursued approaches that
differed from many of the regular processes at Intel,
and moved ahead with the venture before funding
was secured. However, the one element of Croll and
Yoskovitz's prescription that he could not bend was the
requirement for executive buy-in and sponsorship.

Grameen Intel had the endorsement of Craig Barrett
on the Intel side and Muhammad Yunus on Grameen's
end, ensuring support at the highest possible levels of
each organization. As the contract process dragged
on—it would end up taking nearly eighteen months to
finalize the details of the joint venture—Kazi met with
Barrett to brief him on progress and barriers. At the end

of the meeting, Barrett simply asked, 'Where do you need help?' Throughout the process of forming Grameen Intel, Barrett worked in the background to make important connections, provide access to resources, and smooth the way forward.

Meanwhile, Grameen Intel needed to put together its own leadership team to move the new company forward and begin prototype development. Narayan Sundararajan was officially hired as CTO in 2008. At the time, Kazi didn't have approval from Intel Capital to hire anyone at Grameen Intel, since contracts were still being negotiated. Instead, he used his hiring authority as an Intel manager to post the job requirements and make the hire. When Intel Capital challenged Kazi, he told them to go talk to Craig Barrett if they had a problem. 'I knew they wouldn't—but I didn't talk to Craig, either.'

Contract negotiations had now dragged on for more than a year. Yunus didn't believe in hiring expensive lawyers on the Grameen side, but details including entity formation, ownership split between Grameen Trust and Intel Capital, and secondment of Intel managers to Grameen Intel had to be resolved. As Kazi put it,

Western entrepreneurs may have a preconceived notion that it is simply about following the law, but the greater value for Grameen Intel was in setting clear expectations with partners regarding the mission. It forced the team to think through things they would not normally pay attention to. For example, who is paying

for what? Who makes which decisions? How would
you manage the situation under different scenarios?
The predictive, rather than reactive, approach to law
gave the team a clear-headed sense of what needed to
be done.

Ultimately, Grameen Trust and Intel Capital ended
up splitting the voting shares of Grameen Intel. Kazi
hired new employees on his own, and Grameen Intel
Social Business Ltd. was formally established as a new
company. In 2010, the first tranche of money from Intel
Capital and Grameen Trust was released to the new
company. In Bangladesh, however, the challenges were
just beginning.

Because information in Bangladesh was not as
available, and most bureaucratic processes were not
as systematized, as in the West, Kazi and his team
ended up travelling from office to office in search of
answers. Which forms needed to be filled out, where
should they be sent, and who granted approval? It
took Kazi more than a week simply to learn how to
register a company under the Bangladeshi Companies
Act. Grameen Trust was helpful in outlining the
disparate pieces of different processes, but Kazi had
to put them all together to create an operational
company. In response, he began to carefully identify
relevant business processes, create checklists, and
move through them in a deliberate manner, essentially
creating systems the local offices lacked. This included
filing documents with the Registrar of Joint Stock
Companies, obtaining a tax identification number,

trade license, VAT registration, board of investment approval, and permission of Securities and Exchange commission for issuance of new company shares—and this was just half the tasks to get the company established on paper.

Grameen Intel, with Narayan hired as CTO, was already moving ahead with prototype developments and needed to find an office space to house their new local manager, Pavel Hoq, and the future staff. However, even finding a location proved to be challenging. Many businesses simply sublet an apartment—with unclear zoning rules—so Kazi hired an agent to help them find a suitable space. The agent promptly disappeared. While working from Grameen Intel's temporary headquarters (the lobby of a Sheraton hotel), they launched their own search for a space. A ninth-floor office seemed like a fit, until their lawyer discovered that the owner only had a permit to build a seven-floor building. Finally, they rented a space above a grocery store with windows that couldn't be opened because of the dangerous tangle of electrical wires strung directly outside (possibly by Bangladeshi intrapreneurs of a different sort). It wasn't the Sheraton, but it worked.

Accounting and finance systems were another early priority. Kazi wanted clear answers for investors and partners whenever they asked how money was being spent, and he spent months establishing a computerized accounting system. A monthly budget was created to guide spending prioritization, including everything from office snacks all the way to payroll and field implementation, with a shared drive for invoices. Every *taka* had to be tracked because Kazi believed everyone in the organization needed to be accountable for how the shareholders' money was spent.

Finally, they needed talent. As Kazi put it, 'recruiting was probably the hardest area for Grameen Intel'. He and his co-founders saw themselves as problem solvers, and they wanted to find other creative problem solvers. Unfortunately, many of the educational institutions in Bangladesh still relied largely on rote learning, and those few candidates who had developed more creative skillsets were difficult to attract and retain. Grameen Intel found itself competing with profitable telecom companies but could not afford to pay new employees high salaries or bonuses due to limited start-up funds. Instead, they needed to figure out nonfinancial incentives, such as status and career pathways. The brand names of the new company helped, and so did the newly decorated office, which looked like something out of Silicon Valley, at least the interior.

With contracts complete, start-up funding received, and an office established, Kazi's assignment at Grameen Intel was coming to an end. The new company had reached an important period of transition: it had an office, a legal entity, and staff—but the first products had not yet been launched. The company still needed to prove that it could generate both social impact and a financial return, but Kazi would be reassigned unless he could work out an arrangement to remain as CEO. That needed the support of their executive sponsor—but in early 2009, Craig Barrett announced his retirement.

Without an executive sponsor, Kazi said, 'You realize that when there's a problem, you look around and there's nobody. You just have to look at yourself.' Finding a new sponsor within Intel was critical to the success of the venture, especially at the precarious stage of securing buy-in, and Kazi knew that he had to work fast. Barrett introduced him to the head of Intel's CSR office, and Kazi flew to Arizona to meet with her. Unfortunately, she felt that developing and selling a product, even for social benefit, wasn't a fit for their philanthropic model.

Narayan suggested reaching out to John Davies, Vice President of Intel's World Ahead programme. When Davies was presented with the concept, he saw an opportunity to use Grameen Intel to research go-to-market strategies among the world's poorest. As he put it, nearly two-thirds of the world's population had little to no access to the benefits of information technology—but Grameen Intel could change that.

Kazi moved to spending fifty per cent of his time as Grameen Intel CEO, and the rest at Intel's finance division. Other Intel employees, such as Narayan, ended up seconded through World Ahead or other departments and programs. Kazi had secured a new executive sponsor, ongoing roles for key Grameen Intel management, and was ready to prove the model with the launch of their first product, *shumātā*.

Key Lessons:

- Be entrepreneurial no matter where you work.
- Learn the language of investment as a way to secure funding and support for a new concept.
- Intrapreneurship is not a fast process. Be persistent and try multiple approaches.

THREE

Spend Time in the Field and Learn from Small Successes

Narayan Sundararajan, who was now seconded from Intel as Grameen Intel's CTO, grew up in the cosmopolitan port city of Chennai, famous for its filter coffee and Carnatic (South Indian) music festival. To Narayan, the city seemed a blend of ancient and modern, progress and challenge. His family's philosophy was deeply informed by that dialectic, shaped by their own struggles through climbing the financial ladder from lower middle class and their work to alleviate the suffering of others.

Narayan's grandfather was an accountant in the Hindi Prachar Sabha, a national literacy organization led by Mahatma Gandhi. Narayan recalls the oft-repeated story of his grandparents feeding the poor in their own home every day, borrowing rice from neighbours or sharing in hunger if there was not enough for all. His own father, who played in the courtyard of the Hindi Prachar Sabha as a child, now seventy-five and still recalls proudly being lifted up by Mahatma Gandhi, was deeply moved by this philosophy. 'My father, a government forensic scientist, truly was passionate about giving back to the local community, schools and orphanages. He enjoyed working in and for the community immensely.'

Narayan's mother grew up in poverty as the child of a village schoolteacher, but she herself was unable to complete any schooling past the age of eighteen, when she had to start work to support her family. A common refrain from Narayan's mother was, 'If only I knew', lamenting her forgone education—and reiterating her belief that information is the best tool for overcoming poverty. 'We were middle class, but we saw a lot of poverty and many people who didn't have their basic needs met. It's always in your subconscious. I've always thought, "How can I help people who are underprivileged?"'

Narayan would carry that belief in the power of education and information into his educational pursuits, completing his undergraduate degree at the Indian Institute of Technology and his master's and doctorate degrees at Cornell in fibre science and materials science respectively. He worked under professor Kay Obendorf and professor Ober, both of whom he credits with influencing his current career: 'They instilled in me the idea that we should bring technology to where it is relevant and tailor it to meet the needs of people.' That concept stuck with Narayan when he worked at Intel, but it was his brush with a terrible illness that helped him link it to healthcare in developing nations as Grameen Intel's CTO.

Each year, roughly 9 million people contract tuberculosis and 1.5 million die of the disease, the vast majority of them in developing nations. Nearly a quarter of those deaths are among individuals who are HIV positive. Tuberculosis and AIDS are co-morbidities: AIDS weakens the immune system in a way that makes it easier to contract tuberculosis (World Health Organization). During his sabbatical from Intel (which is a fantastic benefit that Intel provides where employees can take 8 weeks of additional paid vacation every seven years), Narayan was in South India helping his wife, a PhD AIDS researcher, film a documentary on AIDS awareness. Part of the trip included visits with AIDS sufferers infected with tuberculosis. When Narayan returned to the United States, he carried a hidden tuberculosis infection with him—one that would not be diagnosed until his now-pregnant wife was about to give birth.

Narayan developed a fever and cough, but the rarity of tuberculosis infections in the US meant that it took ten days to receive a diagnosis. On the day of his child's birth, Narayan was wheeled into surgery for a biopsy. It was three days before he met his son. Although the disease was unlikely to pass between them, the family was monitored for months to ensure that there was no transmission.

Had Narayan been living in a developing nation, it is possible he would never have met his child. Although tuberculosis is easily curable—the vast majority of infected individuals who receive treatment recover,

and drug therapy costs as little as $100—the death rate
remains staggeringly high. How might the sophisticated
medical processes and technologies of the developed
world, the techniques that had saved Narayan's life,
be brought to where they are most relevant and be
tailored to work for the world's poorest? It was a
question that would occupy Narayan in his later
work as Global Program Manager of Intel's Emerging
Markets Healthcare initiative, and then as Grameen
Intel's CTO. In that role, his new job was to focus on
how to address the basic needs of the world's poorest,
a huge group.

In 2015, roughly 3.8 billion people lived on less
than $1,500 a year, a widely accepted definition for
the minimum annual income 'considered necessary
to sustain a decent life' (Prahalad and Hart, 2008)[*].
More than a billion people live on less than $1.25
a day, or approximately $456 a year, the World
Bank's threshold for extreme poverty (World Bank,
2015). The calculation of these numbers is complex.
Incomplete data, calculations of Purchasing Power
Parity (PPP) based on the relative value of different
currencies, and different prices for common goods and
services all complicate an accurate assessment of actual
incomes and the amount needed to meet basic human

---

[*] The authors use the income level set by C.K. Prahalad and
Stuart L. Hart in their article, 'The Fortune at the Bottom of the
Pyramid', in *strategy+business* 26 (2008). The number of those
who earn less than this each year has been updated using the
authors' calculations based on World Bank data for the most
recent years available.

needs. On a smaller scale, the Progress out of Poverty Index, developed by Grameen Foundation, building on indicators used by Grameen Bank, provided a framework for understanding what it means to be 'poor' in different countries based on asset ownership, access to services, income and other indicators that generate a more complete picture.

However, it does not take a sophisticated calculation to understand that around the world vast numbers of people are not able to meet their most basic needs for food, shelter, sanitation, healthcare, and education. This is neither a natural condition of society nor an unavoidable outcome of progress. Yunus believed that 'we accept the idea that we will always have poor people among us, that poverty is part of human destiny. The fact that we accept this notion is precisely why we continue to have the poor' (Yunus, 2008). The data support his argument. China alone lifted 680 million people out of poverty between 1981 and 2010 as a result of economic growth, and the United Nations target for halving extreme poverty between 1990 and 2015 was met five years earlier (*The Economist*, 2013). The eradication of extreme poverty seemed, for the first time in human history, to be achievable. If we believe that we cannot end poverty, we won't; if we believe that we can end poverty, we may.

Grameen Intel, as a social business, had an explicit mission to alleviate poverty by using ICT as a way to improve people's lives around the world. However, the interlocking systems and barriers that create the underlying conditions for poverty offer a nearly infinite set of addressable problems. For a business developing a few prototype concepts meant to tackle these problems, the scope of the problem is simply too large. You have to, as Narayan and Kazi say, 'peel the onion' to find the most basic points of leverage for addressing poverty. Grameen Intel had an initial geographic focus, Bangladesh, based on its partnership with Grameen. They also had a demographic target, working with the 'base of the pyramid', the nearly two-thirds of humanity lacking the income to 'sustain a decent life'. This group was especially prevalent in Bangladesh, with roughly thirty per cent of the nation's 156 million people living below the national poverty line (IFAD, World Bank Group, 2015). Not exactly a narrow focus, but a start.

What was also needed was a clear set of goals for new ICT solutions that could be piloted in Bangladesh but that were applicable worldwide. From a narrow start to broad implementation, following the approach espoused by Yunus. Any set of global goals that Grameen Intel might adopt had to be widely understood, easily communicated, reflect global development priorities, and offer real opportunities for addressing the needs of those at the base of the pyramid. Fortunately for Grameen Intel, every member of the United Nations had recently agreed to such goals.

The Millennium Development Goals (MDGs), adopted in 2000 during 'the largest gathering of world leaders in history', set a list of eight broad goals for addressing global poverty by 2015 (United Nations Millennium Project, 2006):

1. Eradicate extreme poverty and hunger
2. Achieve universal primary education
3. Promote gender equality
4. Reduce child mortality
5. Improve maternal health
6. Combat HIV/AIDS, malaria and other diseases
7. Ensure environmental sustainability
8. Develop a global partnership for development

Each goal was broken down into specific targets that outlined how much progress should be made by 2015. For example, the first goal, to eradicate extreme hunger and poverty, established targets to 'halve, between 1990 and 2015, the proportion of people whose income is less than $1 a day', 'achieve full and productive employment and decent work for all, including women and young people', and 'halve, between 1990 and 2015, the proportion of people who suffer from hunger' (United Nations, 2015). By 2015, the first target had been achieved, the second had made significant progress—with a tripling of the global 'working middle class' living on $4 or more a day—and the third had nearly been met (ibid).

Significant, and sometimes stunning, progress had been made in many other goals, but severe poverty and its effects remained a persistent challenge. By adopting the MDGs as a framework for their efforts, Grameen Intel could utilize existing research and data to understand the scope of specific problems, tap into a global movement to facilitate coordination and funding, and use a common set of measurement tools to evaluate their impact. Grameen Intel decided to focus their initial product and service development on MDGs 1 and 5, eradicating extreme poverty and hunger, and improving maternal health. They later added MDG 2, with products focused on education (see Table 1).

Table 1: MDGs, Targets and Indicators Aligned with Grameen Intel

MDG 1: Eradicate extreme poverty and hunger (aligned with Grameen Intel's mrittikā programmes)
Target 1.A: Halve, between 1990 and 2015, the proportion of people whose income is less than $1.25 a day
1.1 Proportion of population below $1 (PPP) per day
1.1a Proportion of population below national poverty line
1.2 Poverty gap ratio
1.3 Share of poorest quintile in national consumption
Target 1.B: Achieve full and productive employment and decent work for all, including women and young people
1.4 Growth rate of GDP per person employed
1.5 Employment-to-population ratio
1.6 Proportion of employed people living below $1 (PPP) per day
1.7 Proportion of own-account and contributing family workers in total employment
Target 1.C: Halve, between 1990 and 2015, the proportion of people who suffer from hunger
1.8 Prevalence of underweight children under five years of age
1.9 Proportion of population below minimum level of dietary energy consumption

MDG 2: Achieve universal primary education (aligned with Grameen Intel's gSlate application)
Target 2.A: Ensure that, by 2015, children everywhere, boys and girls alike, will be able to complete a full course of primary schooling
2.3 Literacy rate of 15 to 24-year-olds, women and men
MDG 5: Improve maternal health (aligned with Grameen Intel's shumātā programme)
Target 5.A: Reduce by three-quarters, between 1990 and 2015, the maternal mortality ratio
5.1 Maternal mortality ratio
Target 5.B: Achieve, by 2015, universal access to reproductive health
5.5 Antenatal care coverage (at least one visit by a skilled healthcare provider and at least four visits by any provider)

Source: United Nations Millennium Project, 2006

Market and ethnographic research was key to translating Grameen Intel's goals into products or services that met the needs of users on the ground, but shifting the mindset of a tech firm from the allure of new innovations to the pressing needs of poor customers was no small feat. Generally speaking, successful technologists seem to get excited by their own ideas.

Telemedicine is one such idea where doctors would provide remote diagnostics. In Bangladesh, a majority of the doctors live in the cities and serve a well-to-do population segment. Yet the majority of the people in Bangladesh live outside of the major cities. The prevalent idea was to use videoconferencing software, such as

Skype, to connect doctors and overcome the distance barrier. However, Kazi and Narayan's experience clearly showed that most of the doctors already have a backlog of patients in the cities with little time or interest to serve patients in the remote areas with limited ability to pay. Yet, the technologists were super excited about access to broadband and videoconferencing capability on the PC. In a Grameen Intel board meeting that had digressed into a brainstorming session on healthcare, Yunus asked a simple question: 'Let's leave videoconferencing aside for a minute. Cell phones are widespread—why are they not picking up the phone and just talking to a doctor?'

For those in the technology space, market research isn't always seen as necessary to determine the next big thing. We often hear the old chestnut, attributed to Henry Ford, that 'if I had asked my customers what they wanted, they would have said a faster horse'. Tech entrepreneurs easily see the potential of a new innovation for them and other members of the global upper class because they are the end users and understand what will be useful in their own lives. In a way, the developers of technologies are often their own market-research subjects. But when talking about the base of the pyramid, their lives are very different from that of the typically developed world tech entrepreneur, and so there has to be a concentrated effort to fully understand their mindsets, lives and needs.

In order to understand the 'needs', Kazi and Narayan attempted to understand the ways in which healthcare was currently being provided in Bangladesh. Their idea was to surgically insert technology that could simply improve current services, rather than radically designing those services. Yunus connected them to Imamus Sultan, the managing director of Grameen Kalyan, which had sixty health clinics in remote villages. These were small clinics with one doctor and one or two nurses who served the local community. After giving them a quick overview of the clinics, Sultan realized that they actually needed to visit the clinics to get a realistic sense of a village. Sultan offered a minivan with a chauffeur and said they could leave immediately and come back by the end of the day—a day trip to the two closest clinics with at least two hours of driving each way.

One of the clinics was a stand-alone rented house, not more than 1,000 square feet. Upstairs was an apartment for rent. The other clinic looked like a rented shop space, which was next to a tailor's shop. Inside they were fairly sparse. The doctor had a desk with a stethoscope, blood pressure monitor, scale and thermometer. Nurses also had a desk, neatly organized with a register (a logbook that recorded who showed up in the clinics), test tubes, syringes and a small cabinet of essential drugs. There were a dozen or so patients, mostly women, some of them with children. There was a signboard, as soon as you entered, that had a list of services provided and the price for each service.

A conversation with the doctor followed. He mentioned that not more than twenty-five to thirty services were offered—from vaccinations to sonograms for pregnancies. He explained their Safe Motherhood Programme—because many of the pregnant mothers in the village did not come to the clinic voluntarily, mobile healthcare workers went house to house to offer prenatal care, counselling for the mothers, and safe deliveries in the clinic instead of at home. Mothers did have to enrol

in the programme, which typically cost about $4 a year.
This gave them the services at a discount, as well as a
prescription for vitamins and minerals. During visits,
nurses captured vital signs such as pulse, blood pressure
and temperature, and monitored for any pains or other
possible complications.

Although Kazi and Narayan were there to better
understand their operations, and the ways in which
ICT could intervene, all conversations with the doctors
ended with a simple: If they could talk to Mr Sultan
for a transfer to a clinic closer to the city. That wasn't
something Kazi and Narayan could help them with,
but it definitely highlighted the personal incentives that
needed to be part of any solution. Back in the office,
they had multiple rounds of discussions on the best way
to approach healthcare. They talked to more Grameen
Kalyan doctors, local experts and non-governmental
organization (NGO) staff working on similar projects.
Even GE Healthcare had a programme to deploy their
mobile handheld ultrasound equipment in the same
clinics.

With the existing model in mind, Kazi and Narayan
came up with a novel concept on how to better equip
the mobile nurses using ICT coupled with a business
concept. This wouldn't be yet another telemedicine
implementation. Although their new idea also had
no guarantees, it was at least thought through based
on observations on the ground. The concept was that
as mobile workers visited households, they would
electronically register and enter the health data via a
mobile handheld device. The data would immediately
be transmitted to a central database. At a minimum,

this would standardize the steps the nurses took in their regular visits to pregnant clients. Think of this as the nurses capturing clinical survey questions. As the information was collected, it could provide a better assessment on client health and conditions, and depending on the answers, it could flag pregnancies as high risk and send action items automatically to the nurse via SMS. At that time, all information was collected on paper, with no way to aggregate the information and look for trends. This would be a real value addition to Grameen Kalyan's current healthcare services.

The Grameen Intel team went about designing the software and database. There were multiple iterations of the interface on the mobile device—it had to be user-friendly and easily understood. Field-level doctors also had to be comfortable with the set-up. At the same time, they never lost sight of the big picture and the MDGs. This concept would ultimately go towards reducing maternal and child mortality and would address how technology could help meet the challenge. At a tactical level, it would increase enrolment in the programme and use data and analytics for better health outcomes.

The pilot programme was put in motion. They started work in two villages, with four mobile health workers. Each village had a population of approximately 30,000, and their assessment was that, each village had 2,000 or so pregnant mothers. The six-month pilot findings were certainly compelling—120 mothers had registered in the programme, which was six per cent of the total target group. Ongoing monitoring indicated that sixty-three of them (or fifty-five per cent) were at high risk that required follow-up. On the business side, the technology team along with the medical staff explored two different care packages. The first was a nine-month prenatal package that would cover four antenatal visits by the healthcare worker, referral for complications, provide supplements with vitamins, minerals, docosahexaenoic acid and folic acid, and provided an option for transportation facilities during labour. The eighteen-month infant care package, offered after birth, would include nine routine immunizations, automatic SMS reminders, and follow-up home visits for both mother and child.

Kazi and Narayan were excited to have both the technology and the business come together. Additionally, they had the local clinics to provide the brand and credibility for the overall healthcare services. They were simply helping them with technology to increase their social impact.

The six-month project provided proof that an ICT-enabled healthcare approach could work. Grameen Intel didn't try to push the solution but let the experience tell the story for all stakeholders—doctors, mobile healthcare staff and clinic management. The households that received the check-ups were very positive as well. They liked the idea of being connected to a doctor. The mobile healthcare worker liked the automatic prompting of questions and receiving computerized assistance on the steps for the next check-up, especially identifying higher-risk patients who would need more dedicated care. They liked the training that went with it. They also developed a disciplined way to design, implement and improve on the solution. Nick Veldwijk and Sara de Boo, two student interns from the University of Amsterdam, would investigate and coordinate the effectiveness of the solutions.

On completion of the pilot projects, Kazi and Narayan left it up to the local clinic to scale, but after a few months of waiting, they saw only limited uptake. Initially, they assumed that purchasing the set-up, computers, mobile devices and software would be a barrier, which they did hear from the headquarters-level management team. It seemed that the cost of devices needed to be lower, but it was difficult to assess the target price point and/or features vs cost trade-offs. Therefore, like any good corporate managers, they went about documenting their findings and developing a detailed report. At the end of this assessment, they came to some very basic conclusions that contradicted this assessment. The cost of the solution was not a barrier, provided there was a way to recoup the costs through more enrolment in the healthcare programme. But often it's the basic things that are overlooked, simply because we do not live the lives of those we are trying to impact.

First was the healthcare worker at the point of delivery. Transitioning to a paperless system had its challenges. There was a personal barrier, similar to those who like taking notes with a pen and notebook. The change is quite dramatic if you are asked to shift to, for example, note-taking software. How many of us in the West have been able to transition to online notes? They thought data entry using a keyboard was cumbersome and worried that all that work simply disappeared after hitting 'submit'. Previously, there would be a stack of paper to show how much work they did in a given day. Now they didn't even have that. But, perhaps most importantly, it was also the issue of having to do both the note register-based system as well as mobile phone based technology solution that proved very cumbersome for the health workers even though it would be only for the pilot period but gave the perception that this was way too much work!

Second, there was the doctor—good luck orienting him or her to now sit in front of a computer, looking at data instead of personally interacting with a patient. In addition, they may have already been lobbying for a transfer to a city-based assignment (where life was better and pay was higher), and were not invested in a long-term improvement of the clinic. They remained on the same monthly salary with or without an ICT-based healthcare system. Also, they could be picky even when convinced to use a computer. Grameen Intel provided one of the doctors a prototype of a $100 laptop they were working on for the emerging market. The screen was smaller than a typical laptop and the keyboard was more compact with smaller keys. The doctor returned the low-cost laptop and asked for a 'real laptop' that was faster, thinner, and had a larger screen.

Third is the end beneficiary. Here the barrier was a little more subtle but boiled down to understanding the value of preventive care. Most of the healthcare that Kazi and Narayan had observed was reactive in nature. You went to the doctor when you had a problem. Seeing the value of regular monitoring and taking vitamins was a little abstract, given typical levels of education and the ready availability of elders in the household eager to give advice for free.

It's virtually impossible for those who haven't lived those lives to come up with such a compelling scenario with just a technology focus and without understanding all the people involved and their motivations. What are their day-to-day struggles, their economic priorities, their cultural milieu? What a Western business person considers to be a rational decision-making process may not apply because local imperatives are very different. A farmer considers a best practice to be what his father or grandfather did for decades. Why would he trust a young, hotshot entrepreneur providing a soil-testing service and second-guessing their usual way of doing things? Or, why would a pregnant mother listen to a twenty-eight-year-old mobile healthcare worker when her mother-in-law, in her fifties, already has five children of her own and offers contradictory advice?

At the core of the issue is a lack of education, and although that couldn't be solved quickly, exposure to early impacts and convincing results was a starting point. Grameen Intel needed to spearhead a number of pilot projects to demonstrate results, gain trust and provide information to help iterate the next version of each prototype. A key tenet of social business is that the poor are not simply beneficiaries but customers worthy of attention, consideration, and quality products and services no less than the richest consumers in developed nations. These products and services should bring those struggling with poverty a tangible benefit, ideally empowering them as franchise owners or entrepreneurs at the same time, thereby meeting one, or both, of Yunus's social business requirements. Designing such a product or service can only be done in concert with the potential end users and customers, an approach now embraced both by Silicon Valley—through Steve Blank's Customer Development Process and the Lean Startup movement it informed—and by social enterprises and nonprofits, through Human-Centred Design (HCD), community co-creation, public interest design, or any of the other sector-specific names for similar processes.

IDEO.org's HCD approach, developed in concert with International Development Enterprises, outlines both the process and goals for a social entrepreneur launching a new venture. The 'Hear-Create-Deliver' sequence first emphasizes deep engagement with affected communities, learning from eventual customers or end users as well as experts, as a guide to understanding the problem at hand and designing an effective solution. Any such solution should then be created as an iterative prototype that can be tested with customers, a process similar to the 'build-measure-learn' loop from Eric Ries' *The Lean Startup* that so many traditional entrepreneurs now practice (or say they do). Once the prototype solution is proven, a business model is designed to effectively deliver it over time.

Human-Centred Design emphasizes that the goal of this process is to create an effective solution that is also feasible, desirable, and viable; that is, technologically achievable, clearly wanted by customers and beneficiaries, and financially sustainable over long term. Financial viability is often driven by the technical feasibility of a solution (more complicated solutions tend to be more expensive to design, deliver, and maintain) and its desirability to customers (are they willing to pay for it?). Again, the poor are not just beneficiaries but also customers. They have money to spend, albeit not much, which makes it all the more important that what is being sold to them is high-quality and durable, affordable (perhaps with a microloan), and meets a basic need or helps them generate more income.

The cost of not treating the poor as customers who deserve the best was very clear to Narayan. His tuberculosis episode could have easily been fatal had he been one of the billion people who live in extreme poverty. Working on Grameen Intel's healthcare approach was a way to bring his technical expertise to bear on an issue of personal importance, a deep alignment of purpose and work. With their next product, a soil-testing application that could be used by micro-franchisees to help their neighbours and earn themselves an income, they would work to tackle poverty itself, not just its symptoms.

Key Lessons:

- Start with the wants and needs of your end user.
- Adopt a 'beginner's mindset': be curious and open to new information, while rejecting preconceived ideas about your users.
- Going with what is cheap or available now can backfire in the long run.
- You have to work on big ideas (such as global goals), but you also have to build based on ground-level experience, listening and trying things out step by step.

FOUR

Keep Solutions Real

Saphy Pon is a rice farmer in Cambodia. His salary is a few hundred dollars per year. He used to plough his paddy with a water buffalo, but recently he purchased a gas-powered ploughing machine. This gives him better rice yields, which now makes some school supplies affordable for his children—only a few incremental dollars, but a big change in the economic future of his children. Delwar Mira has been a farmer in Bangladesh for over twenty years. He speaks proudly of his land and how he cultivates rice: he prepares his fields prior to a crop cycle through repeated ploughing, which turns over the upper layer of the soil, bringing fresh nutrients to the surface. It also aerates the soil and allows it to hold moisture better. This is all done by manual labour on his small piece of land. Most of his hard work goes to produce food for his own family, and there simply isn't sufficient output left to bring in additional income. For

46

him, higher production simply means adequate food for his family.

More than one billion people worldwide rely on agriculture for their employment (FAO, 2012). Paradoxically, these farmers and their families make up a disproportionate share of those suffering from hunger and are also more likely to be poor than urban residents (World Food Programme, 2015). Subsistence farmers often struggle to produce enough food for their own families or to earn enough from their crop to purchase food due to a host of challenges: not enough land or barely arable land; lack of access or inability to pay for essential inputs (seeds, fertilizers and equipment); natural disasters and changing climate patterns; limited labour availability due to family illness or migration; warfare and political instability; no title to their land; limited access to markets where they could sell extra produce, either from poor infrastructure, distance, or not owning an adequate vehicle; lack of market knowledge on prices and distribution; no access to credit to purchase new family assets, such as livestock . . . the list is nearly endless.

Unfortunately, many of those same conditions that contribute to the intersection of hunger and poverty among the world's farmers and rural populations also serve as barriers to development. The problems are more acute in countries like India and Bangladesh, which along with China has the majority of the world's farmers, although not necessarily a majority of the world's agricultural lands. As populations increased, the division of family lands over successive generations continued to shrink farm sizes, which diminished income opportunities for each farmer. Most of the farming population in this part of the world live on less than $3.50/day.

A washed-out dirt road that limits transport of products to the local market also restricts health workers access to the village. The same government corruption or bureaucracy that restricts land ownership may inhibit a social enterprise from securing a business licence. An effective solution is not enough; to ensure widespread adoption in the areas where it is most needed, any new product or service introduced by a social enterprise also needs an effective business model.

As entrepreneurship guru Steve Blank succinctly puts it, 'A business model describes how your company creates, delivers and captures value' (Blank, 2012). The type of value created, and for whom, varies by organization. J. Gregory Dees, whose definition of social entrepreneurship is built on a century of entrepreneurial theory and definitions, explains it thus: 'Entrepreneurship is about value creation, but it doesn't have to be financial value' (Dees, 2012). All organizations create multiple types of value; a traditional for-profit corporation might privilege financial value creation for shareholders, while a social business emphasizes the generation of tangible social value for the poor.

Value creation to benefit those in poverty historically has been philanthropic or subsidy-driven, with handouts paid directly to farmers as supplemental income or subsidized fertilizers and other inputs, reducing their cost burden. Many of the NGOs Grameen Intel had worked with were project driven, for example, by training farmers in better agricultural practices, or by demonstrating to farmers ways to prevent pests from destroying their crops. Many charitable foundations set objectives and implementation policies then provide funding but leave it to other organizations to do the real work on the ground. These programmes are typically not sustainable and are short in duration; projects stop when the money runs out.

When social businesses try to enter the field with new products, their approach to value creation is different. In addition to non-financial value, the social business has to survive if it is to make a lasting impact. It may not be driven by profits, but needs to generate enough revenue to recoup costs, at a minimum. The social business also has to serve multiple stakeholders. In the case of Grameen Intel, Grameen was clearly focused on ways to improve the livelihoods of the poor. Intel wanted to ensure that their R&D was being put to good use and actual products were being developed and used in the field. The investors, on the other hand, wanted to ensure that the enterprise was being run in the most cost-effective way possible and that there was a path to financial sustainability. Social business needs to have a revenue or cost-recovery model, with a real service, preferably embedding social goals in their business model.

Of course, modelling how a social enterprise simultaneously generates different types of value for its various stakeholders can be challenging. Alexander Osterwalder and Yves Pigneur's Business Model Canvas, a fixture in many entrepreneurship courses and workshops, offers a much easier way to map value creation than a business plan, which tends to be geared more towards investors than managers. The canvas depicts in a simple graphic how an organization 'creates, delivers and captures' value. One side of the canvas shows internal operations, another external marketing and engagement, with both halves linked by the concept of a 'value proposition'. For a social business, that core value proposition may be social or environmental in nature.

In Grameen Intel's case, they tracked value creation with three key indicators: product milestones (adding value for customers and investors), social impact (creating value for beneficiaries and partners) and financial success (generating value for staff and investors). In turn, these three indicators drove the business model and tied into the MDGs linked to their impact.

---

* A quick note on terminology: throughout the book, 'beneficiaries' is used to describe individuals who benefit from a product or service but don't always pay for it; 'end users' describes those who use it but may or may not benefit directly from it; and 'customers' typically includes both groups.

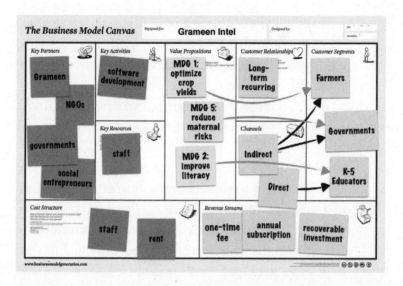

One example was Grameen Intel's tool to increase crop yields and income for farmers through better crop planning via a computerized soil assessment (described in more detail later in this chapter). The core value proposition was poverty alleviation through optimized crop yields, which drove specific indicators. 'Product milestones' included a prototype in six months and a field-usable product in twelve to eighteen months. The 'social impact' included tracking how many organizations were using the product and how many farmers were provided with a soil-testing service. The 'financial success' included how many software licences were actually sold and distributed. These three indicators provided discipline in execution, outcomes and timeline, and gave a sense of whether the overall business model, designed to deliver on that core value proposition, was functioning as planned.

One way to achieve this is to not lose sight of the fact that a single solution needs to start with one problem, one customer and, perhaps, in one village. The challenge is to make this attractive to the one person, otherwise it does not 'go viral'. It was the American business guru who said, 'The purpose of a business is to create a customer.'

There also needed to be a business model for the customer. It was not feasible for a farmer to purchase devices; many of them could not afford it, but more importantly they would not be able to decipher the technical information delivered by the device. Instead, the idea was to generate small businesses where a local entrepreneur would provide local testing services. Many companies in the social impact space, start too broad, don't follow this 'rule of one', and end up dabbling in a lot of theoretical possibilities.

Grameen Intel had learnt this lesson well when its information kiosk concept was rejected. The kiosk did not deliver enough value to potential end users, and the company would not be able to capture enough of that value in payments to ensure financial success. As Kazi and Narayan explored other potential solutions for alleviating poverty and hunger in rural areas—where two-thirds of Bangladesh's population lived—it was clear that they needed to develop a working business model that could be tested at the prototype stage. How would the solution create value by reducing poverty or hunger, how would it deliver that value through sales and distribution, and how would it capture that value through payments?

The team narrowed in on agriculture for the new product based on its clear potential for addressing the MDGs the company prioritized. As they conducted research in rural farming communities in Bangladesh— the 'hear' phase in Human-Centred Design's hear-create-deliver cycle—it became apparent that this was an area rich in information. Farmers needed to understand the condition of the soil, nutrient levels, harvest timing, fertilizer application intervals and amounts, seed types, and a dozen other variables. But most of the farmers they met during field research didn't even know how to read or write. How was it they were dealing with such a complex process on a day-to-day basis?

The simple answer is that they weren't. Very little was known about scientific ways to improve crop yields at a village level. Some of the farmers mentioned government agricultural extension officers they could receive information from, but Kazi and Narayan barely found few of them. When they finally managed to locate these extension officers and asked them about soil testing, one possible avenue of new product design, the officers described centres where the farmers could send soil samples. However, for most farmers these centres were far away, and they knew little about how to conduct such sampling, the benefits of the tests, or what the tests would cost.

The Government of Bangladesh had centralized expertise in specific locations and among certain individuals, but actual farmers had very little access because there was no business model for disseminating that information or demonstrating its value. Kazi and

Narayan hit on a simple solution: What if they took that centralized information and decentralized in a way that would be accessible at a local level? How could they create a business model to deploy that information where it was needed, when it was needed, in the most effective way possible?

They knew they were tackling a huge problem by seeking to address poverty and hunger through agricultural services, and they sought to reduce that problem to specific issues that farmers would find relatable (and that the company would find tractable). Through Srinivas Garudachar, one of the first Intel employees assigned to Grameen Intel, Kazi and Narayan were introduced to social entrepreneur K.C. Mishra. In Odisha state in eastern India, Mishra had previously worked with the government on agricultural lending initiatives and had collaborated with the Odisha University of Agriculture and Technology. He was also the founder of eKutir, a social enterprise focused on rural development in India, which would later lead to his recognition as an Ashoka Fellow—one of the highest honours a social entrepreneur can receive.

Mishra explained that apps for weather forecasts and market prices were already available, but that there was no easy software solution for soil testing, despite its importance to subsistence farmers. Kazi and Narayan saw that a soil-testing application could be an excellent, unaddressed way to expand the centralized knowledge of government workers and centres for the benefit of farmers. Many farmers in developing nations had little to no access to soil-testing services, which meant that they tended to over apply chemical fertilizers and hope for the best. For impoverished farmers, the cost of fertilizer was a major outlay, and any way to help them reduce application without affecting crop yields would boost family incomes. In addition, over-application of fertilizers led to soil degradation and water pollution, reducing yields in the long term and affecting the health of anyone drinking from contaminated water sources. By simply providing accurate information on soil macronutrients and recommending a specific amount of fertilizer, an app could generate significant social and environmental benefits.

Based on conversations with experts, Kazi and Narayan identified several key soil macronutrients and indicators the testing service should focus on:

- Nitrogen (deficiency speeds up the ageing of leaves)
- Phosphorus (deficiency causes purpling of leaves)
- Potassium (deficiency weakens stems and branches)
- pH (alkaline soil can be toxic to plants, and overly acidic soil lowers nutrient uptake)
- Organic Carbon (important for soil fertility)

Coupled with information on land use and agro-ecological zones, an analysis of these indicators could provide basic recommendations for type and amount of fertilizer to be applied for specific crops. Grameen Intel's new software engineers began creating a mobile software application for the ubiquitous Android platform that mapped appropriate nutrient levels by region, with extensive help from academic researchers.

eAgro

A professor from a local university worked with them to design the algorithm. Kazi and Narayan learnt that two faculty members from Cornell University were conducting research in Dhaka and soon had them at the new office to demonstrate the prototype software. The Cornell faculty provided guidance, additional research materials, and connections to four PhD students who flew out to assist with the project. The students spent several weeks in Bangladesh analysing the software, talking to farmers in the field, and making improvements based on end-user feedback. They were well along in the 'create' phase of design, updating and improving the product based on deep engagement with both experts and users.

The initial software application, called *mrittikā* or 'mother Earth', didn't actually test the soil. Instead, it provided a quick way to analyse the results of inexpensive soil tests. For the type of soil-test kits used in Bangladesh, samples are taken from a farmer's field using well known prescribed procedures, placed into pipettes preloaded with different chemicals, and the resulting colour of the samples is compared to a chart that enables quick evaluation of key indicators and macronutrient levels. These are similar to the home-testing kits used by American or European home gardeners, or at least the ambitious ones. The results of such tests would then be entered into the app, which would recommend the appropriate type and amount of fertilizer for the intended crop. Greater detail in the recommendation could be enabled by entering the generic type of soil, location, irrigation type and other factors that were built in as the software went through multiple iterations.

It quickly became clear that with the information entered from soil-testing kits, a mobile software application could do much more than simply recommend the appropriate type and amount of fertilizer. Kazi and Narayan hit on the idea of displaying the cheapest local places to purchase recommended fertilizer, until Muhammad Yunus reminded them that in Bangladesh fertilizer prices were controlled by the government. But in other countries, this was still an important guidance factor that farmers appreciate. Other concepts, however, proved more workable, and *mrittikā* quickly became the first in a suite of mobile software tools called 'eAgro'. In addition to soil testing, the farmers also needed help to select seeds, control pests and connect to potential buyers after the harvest. Each service was a module in the eAgro software suite with a local name.

The *ankur* application used soil type, location and soil test results among other inputs to recommend seed types for a selected crop, and also provided lists of local sellers and fair prices (since seeds were not regulated by the government). This was meant to increase farm yields, and therefore incomes and food, while also enabling cost savings at the beginning of the season.

Protikār provided information on preventative pest control measures, and failing that, recommended pesticide types and amounts along with safe application procedures. This not only generated cost savings for farmers, which would hopefully serve to entice them to use the product but also offered a host of ancillary benefits. In developing nations, where pesticide ingredients and usage are often less regulated than in developed regions, reducing overuse and ensuring safe application is extremely important to protect the health of farmers, their families, their communities and local ecosystems.

Vistār connected farmers directly to buyers online, providing clear information on market prices and bypassing middlemen. By disintermediating the flow of crops from farmer to buyer, the farmers could capture more of the value that previously had gone to middlemen, and benefit from information that was often withheld from them by those intermediaries.

Moving into the 'deliver' phase, the business model designed by Grameen Intel was intended to spread adoption by making the application available to franchisees. These might be local sellers of agricultural inputs who were already well known in the community. Software licences were sold at $10 apiece and training was offered to franchisees. They would provide the soil-test kits and testing services to their communities for a fee, which created an income opportunity for them, generated cost savings for farmers utilizing the service, and enabled more effective last-mile distribution than a centrally managed approach. Because soil testing needed to be redone before each crop cycle, it also created a recurring revenue stream—enabling Grameen Intel to effectively capture the value that they created and their franchisees delivered. But how could they prove to farmers that they were actually creating value for them? They followed Yunus's advice:

> *I urge anyone who has an idea for a social business to start work on it as soon as possible. Even if it improves life for only five people—by lifting them out of poverty, providing them with a home, or bringing them affordable healthcare—it is worth undertaking. It's not necessary to wait to see the impact on millions of people. 'Millions' is a big number. If your work has a positive impact on five or ten people, you have invented a seed. Now you can plant it a million times* (2010).

There were more than one billion farmers to help, but they didn't have the scale or money to reach out to most of them. So why not start with one village and, even better, one farmer? If Kazi and Narayan could convince one farmer at a time, this would hopefully break down some of the cultural barriers to change and help them develop a repeatable solution for all. So, they asked a farmer to divide up his land into two parts: one where he would grow the crop his own way, as he had always done, and the other using suggestions from their software to see if there was a difference.

Working with eKutir in Odisha, Grameen Intel set up a series of small-scale tests with individual farmers. The results were striking. By reducing fertilizer costs, purchasing higher-quality and higher-yielding seeds, and adjusting labour as a result of better knowledge, the four farmers who participated in the test were able to raise their net farming income between thirty per cent and 280 per cent over the course of a year—despite a small increase in their outlays for inputs and services.

Even the least successful test result provided an interesting example. Arjun Nayak, one of the farmers in the study, grew vegetables on two and a half acres of land in rural Odisha. Through the test, he was connected to vetted seed providers at the beginning of the year, rather than purchasing from the usual middleman, and paid slightly more for those inputs. However, purchasing from a reputable seller enabled him to boost seed-germination rates from thirty per cent to more than eighty per cent. Nayak paid less for fertilizer based on soil-testing results and analysis and was able to reduce the amount of time he spent tending to the field after he changed to higher-quality more appropriate seed varieties saving both time and money. He also saved money on pesticides, following advice tailored to his land and crop types. At the end of the year, Nayak boosted his farm's production by fifteen per cent, increased sales by forty-three per cent, and improved his overall net income by fifty-nine per cent.

Although Grameen Intel focused the initial app design on a huge issue—eradicating poverty by helping rural farmers—it was important to reduce that to one specific problem. With the help of experts and users the immediate problem was clearly defined as the impact of soil nutrients on agricultural productivity. That enabled them to tackle the solution head-on. Starting with the simplest possible approach, and building on it iteratively, helped them avoid the temptation to add in unnecessary bells and whistles or get lost in the overarching problem. Panels, studies and reports provide a clear direction, but can cause those seeking a solution to lose sight of the most fundamental starting point: the condition of the soil and how that affects the livelihoods, and lives, of farmers like Arjun Nayak and his family.

Key Lessons:

- Solutions need to address real information needs.
- Solutions need to enable real business transactions.
- Solutions need to be relevant and sustainable at the local level.
- The role of the intermediary, the local service provider, is critical.

FIVE

Less Is More, Focus Is Key

In Bangladesh, maternal and infant mortality rates place it among the bottom fifty countries worldwide, worsened by a critical lack of healthcare access. Fewer than half of pregnant women receive any prenatal care, and only one-third of births have a trained healthcare professional present (World Health Organization, 2016). Among the poor, outcomes are even worse: less than one in ten women in the poorest twenty per cent of the population receive assistance from any healthcare professional during birth (Ahmed, 2015).

Bangladesh's government-managed urban hospitals and community clinics (each divided among two competing bureaucracies) lack the supplies, staff and culture to effectively serve the population, while private providers are clustered in the cities and unaffordable for many. Filling the gap in rural areas, and among the poor, are a range of traditional healers and NGOs.

These NGOs and national campaigns have been credited with some impressive reductions in infectious diseases, diarrhoea, and mother and child mortality that nearly met the 2015 targets for the related MDGs (Ibid).

Unfortunately, Bangladesh was close to meeting MDG 5, to reduce maternal mortality by seventy-five per cent, only because it had started from a much higher ratio than other countries (Government of Bangladesh, 2015). Grameen Intel sought to hasten progress in this area by developing a new IT solution for maternal health. To do so, they continued to reach out to Grameen Kalyan, part of the Grameen network. Some of the challenges in designing a healthcare solution and associated issues with having a sustainable business model have been highlighted in Chapter 3. However, both Grameen Kalyan managing director Imamus Sultan and Muhammad Yunus wanted Grameen Intel to continue to assess what could be done for maternal care. They believed the poor, like any of us, would do whatever it took to invest in their children. It was important for the next generation to have a better life, something that could be achieved by helping the current generation. After Grameen Intel's initial rapid prototyping of a solution and limited implementation in two clinics, they were ready to build on their prototype to create a more effective solution.

Grameen Kalyan had originally been established to serve Grameen Bank borrowers with healthcare. For the equivalent of $2, anyone could join an annual programme that entitled them to receive discounted care at the clinics. By 2016, Grameen Kalyan operated more than eighty-five clinics across the country, with service regions covering 3.5 million people (Grameen Kalyan, 2016). Each service region spanned between thirty-six and forty-two square kilometres in area, designed to reach approximately 30,000 to 40,000 people. All the clinics had a pharmacy with essential drugs and a mini-laboratory for basic diagnostic tests, addressing some of the most common failings of public clinics.

Managing director Sultan offered Kazi and Narayan again a company microbus to visit two of the clinics in the Savar district on the outskirts of Dhaka. Like the last time, Sultan agreed to provide a driver and guide, but this time Grameen Intel had to pay for gas. Sultan, with his acute business sense, wanted to reduce the burden of a 'casual' trip on those who could barely pay the premiums for their healthcare. The same district would later become infamous after a garment factory fire in 2012 that killed more than 100 workers (Ross and Mosk, 2012) and a building collapse in 2013 that led to the deaths of more than 1,000 (Thomas, 2018)—incidents that shed light on the working conditions and lives of the inhabitants.

When Kazi and Narayan set out to visit the clinics, they reflected again on the barriers they saw in their previous implementation—personal challenges faced by the front-line nurses in transitioning from paper to electronic records, a lack of interest from doctors, and patients' difficulties in understanding the value of preventive care. When presented with the idea, clinic staff had initially showed interest, and at the corporate level there was no lack of ideas, but there was little progress on implementation. Another trip, for another round of discovery, would perhaps lead to some critical insights.

The trip from downtown Dhaka to the first clinic, on a warm summer day, like the last time, took nearly three hours. The dusty road was jammed with trucks, buses, cars and pedestrians, in sharp contrast to the placid rice paddies stretching to the horizon on both sides. From time to time they passed isolated shops, village offices or schools in the fields. The microbus only slowed down for townships, a cluster of concrete shops around an open-air bazaar where farmers sold produce and cattle. Men wearing shirts and lungis (a short sarong tied around the waist) surged back and forth across the road.

The first clinic had white concrete walls and a tin roof. Similar to their previous trips, the little building, no more than 600 square feet, housed a front reception, a doctor's office, a pharmacy and a delivery room. A poster on the wall showed a cheerful nurse with a stethoscope examining a happy woman in a colourful sari. Another promised good medical treatment for a woman and her child. The clinic was staffed by a doctor, a nurse and a pharmacy manager. The nurse, sitting at the reception, had a syringe at hand. A board on the desk listed a menu of services—sonograms, check-ups, vaccinations—that demonstrated the Grameen approach of starting with the most basic items that people could not otherwise access.

Kazi and Narayan met the village doctor, likely in his thirties, who wore slacks, a shirt and a pair of leather sandals. He told them that he grew up in the village but went to the city for his education. His only familiarity with technology was his cell phone and the sonogram equipment. He briefed them on the healthcare plan, his staff and their challenges. This time, Kazi and Narayan wanted to collect more information on possible financial incentives, and the doctor told them he made the equivalent of $200 per month, and he wanted to head back to the city to make more money. This, in itself, wasn't unusual, based on their prior visits.

At the second clinic, the doctor, who was a recent graduate from the local medical school, spoke English. The additional insight he provided was that most patients were not well educated, so writing down a prescription meant they could only understand the doctor's instructions with the help of someone in the household who could read and write.

From conversations at both clinics, Kazi and Narayan learnt three key lessons during their second trip: offerings didn't have to be complex because locals still needed the most fundamental and basic services; finding a local doctor and retaining him/her in a remote village continued to be difficult; when dealing with a customer base with low literacy, continuous follow-up with patients was a must.

The reader will recall that many existing technology solutions tried to address the problem of retention by using telemedicine, connecting rural patients with a doctor in the city via Skype. Unfortunately, there was also a shortage of doctors working with poor clients in the cities, since they had more than enough clients who were willing to pay (and stand in line for it). In Bangladesh, ninety-eight per cent of the doctors lived in urban areas, which meant that only two per cent of them served the seventy per cent of the population that lived in rural areas. A city doctor didn't have any incentive to service village communities.

Sultan's alternate idea on this round was to set up a call centre with dedicated doctors. That way they could be paid a decent salary and would not have to venture outside the cities where they preferred to live. But staffing a call centre with doctors would be a challenge given the existing shortage. Training mobile nurses, who already lived in the local communities, to provide additional services seemed to be the only viable solution. To determine the right approach, though, more research was needed. In keeping with the Human-Centred Design approach, Kazi and Narayan would supplement their personal conversations with ethnographic research and interviews with experts.

The discussion in Grameen Intel's next board meeting was equally challenging and a good case study of 'constructive confrontation'. One board member, who shall remain nameless, questioned why some members of the team deserved their salary given the slow progress on healthcare initiatives, where the need for technology was so obvious. 'Where was the "business" in social business?' Truth be told, given all the challenges in healthcare, Kazi and Narayan simply did not have clarity on how to best go about a simple business offering.

One area that was clear from their previous experience and trips was that there were multiple players involved in the delivery of healthcare, making it unclear who was accountable for success or failure at an individual level. What was the management incentive, accountability and urgency to get the job done? The delivery model ended up being incredibly complex and so did the current business model. Yet when they stepped back, the healthcare needs for the underserved were obvious: they needed to expand access, improve clinical outcomes and do it in a cost-effective way. They decided to not give up, learn from their earlier setbacks and try again.

Shortly after the trip, Kazi was introduced to Omar Ishrak, then CEO of GE Healthcare Systems and later CEO of Medtronics, who was in Portland, Oregon, to visit his daughter at Reed College. Ishrak, who grew up in Bangladesh, was already working with Yunus to deploy GE's new handheld sonogram equipment there. During a lunch meeting in a mutual friend's backyard, Ishrak impressed on Kazi the need to be more aggressive with Grameen Intel's proposed solution, rather than experimenting behind the scenes. He told Kazi, 'You should get the health division at Intel involved in a big way.' Unfortunately, Grameen Intel's challenge in working with Intel's health division was that their current software targeted for the clinics wouldn't make any money in the short term. They were focused on large hospitals buying millions of dollars of technology a year—not exactly the typical customers of a rurally focused social business.

Ishrak shared his insight on working with healthcare technologies in developing nations, advice which he later summarized in a talk at Johns Hopkins. In addition to the technological goals of improving clinical outcomes, there should also be a clear economic value and educational opportunity for patients. A pregnant woman might wonder, will I really have a healthier birth and save my life and my child's by using this service? The benefits needed to be made clear through education.

Furthermore, when working with the underserved, clinics that tried to do everything often failed to move the needle. Spreading their efforts resulted in less impact in any one area. Instead, it was important to start with a prevalent disease. Perhaps even maternal health was too broad a problem. This linked back to the economic value and educational opportunity of an intervention: Do patients understand the need? Can they learn more about how to improve their own health, or that of their family? These are easier to convey for a relatively common ailment or the prevention of a very specific disease.

Using appropriate delivery mechanisms was another piece of advice. Front-line delivery in many developing nations is marked by a shortage of doctors, so training mobile nurses and other agents is important for creating real impact. This was consistent with Kazi and Narayan's prior observations. Finally, Ishrak believed that every actor in the value chain had to be financially incentivized to participate—a need clearly illustrated by Bangladeshi doctors' flight to the cities. Grameen Intel's ethnographic research would confirm many of these insights with additional data.

Life in a Village

The social business conducted studies in three categories: health and wellness with an Indian firm, agriculture using a local company in Bangladesh, and wearable devices. The agriculture study covered two villages: Gorai, a large village, and Bastail, a small village nine kilometres away. The villages were picked for their close proximity to Grameen clinics (run by a separate arm of Grameen Healthcare), so that Grameen Intel could work with the clinics on technology intervention at a local level as they better understood customer needs. The villages were also selected for their differences in size and variation in village economies, since Kazi and Narayan wanted to understand different conditions affecting health-seeking behaviour.

Gorai's economy was primarily based on agriculture and similar activities—farming, fishing, diaries and poultry—with some service work in factory mills. House rentals, general trading, sand collection from the riverbed, and brick-kiln work were other major economic activities in this larger village. The researchers found that milk producers, of which there were between thirty and forty in the village, used mobile phones to collect information about daily prices from traders in nearby markets. This information helped inform sales to both buyers in the local market and traders from outside the village.

Weekly *haats*, or farmers' markets, were integral parts of the village economy where producers and sellers engaged in business transactions. Haats were held twice a week in both villages. Major products like rice, sugar cane, potatoes, fruits and vegetables, fish, betel leaves, meat and poultry were traded in haats. Most sellers came from villages within about eight kilometres, whereas traders/buyers came from towns or villages up to fifteen kilometres away.

Gorai's industrial mills were primarily engaged in textile production (weaving, spinning), manufacturing bicycle parts, and bay leaf oil extraction, which provided regular employment to villagers and outsiders who migrated there in search of jobs. The migrant population stayed in rented houses, which provided a good source of income for locals. Remittances from relatives working abroad were another major income stream for the villagers of Bastail. Money earned in this way was generally remitted through government banks where the migrant and a family member held a joint account. When earnings were deposited, the migrant would inform his family through a text message and they would go to the bank to make a withdrawal. This money was mostly used for loan repayment and asset building.

The remittances were part of a larger trend in villages across the region and around the world. In 2017, nearly $69 billion in remittances were sent back to India by migrants working abroad and almost $13.5 billion dollars were sent to Bangladesh in the same way (Pew Research Center, 2019). The research firm employed by Grameen Intel found that in Bastail alone at least one member from sixty per cent of the families had migrated abroad. Most of them left for Singapore, Italy, London, Abu Dhabi and Bahrain. Those leaving were typically semi-skilled workers, such as mechanics and masons, or unskilled workers, such as general labourers and cleaners.

Many of the migrant workers had attended a local primary school and had the basic ability to read and write in their local language. They would hear from their fellow villagers the income potential of working abroad. They would then contact a broker in the city who recruited labourers for companies abroad. But there would be a one-time payment to cover the cost of migration and the broker's fees. It was astronomical for these families, who would often spend 100,000 to 150,000 taka—roughly $1,275 to $1,900—to send one person abroad. These costs included obtaining a visa, paying for travel and facilitating job training. The money was generally borrowed from friends or neighbours at a ten per cent interest rate, which was reasonable when compared to the rates imposed by informal lenders. The minimum monthly income of migrants was around 20,000 taka, compared to 1,500 to 3,000 taka for family members lucky enough to secure a job in a local factory or mill. Migrants usually spent 5,000 to 7,000 taka of this income each month, remitting the rest home every few months. Given the relatively low risk of the investment, it was clear why friends and neighbours were willing to lend money for migration. For low- and semi-skilled individuals seeking to migrate, and for their families, this investment had an extremely high return and short payback period compared to the other, limited opportunities at hand.

Those local opportunities included starting a business, such as a shop or poultry-raising operation, constructing a small house for rent, participating in festivals, or amassing a marriage dowry. Loans were made to female family members (men had worse repayment odds) by microlenders such as Grameen Bank, BRAC, ASA (Association for Social Advancement) and UDAY (Ujwal DISCOM Assurance Yojana). The loan procedure itself was simple, with no collateral or security required, and repayment typically completed in a year.

Among the farmers Grameen Intel's ethnographic team spoke to, monthly household expenditures of 5,000 to 7,000 taka were broken down as follows: sixty per cent of income spent on food; ten per cent on education; ten per cent on health; ten per cent on electricity, mobile phones, clothes and entertainment; five per cent on festivals; and five per cent on savings. Some families had additional income sources, with remittances from abroad or family members working in the city, which enabled them to save for major health expenses, as a kind of informal insurance, for school admission and books for children, and for future festivals. Some purchased land or kept money in a savings account as part of a lending agreement.

Mobile phones were common in both villages. Every family with a member working abroad had a phone, which was typically used to communicate with migrants, other relatives and friends for business or transactional purposes. Apart from these calls, phones were also utilized as radios, calculators, watches and alarm clocks, serving an array of functions and replacing a set of expensive items with a single portable device. Since most of these were 'dumb' phones without internet connectivity, online access was limited to two internet cafes in Gorai, typically used only by village youth seeking jobs or accessing test results. Government officials and migrants were the only adults familiar with various information technology services or applications.

Healthcare access was limited. Basic services were provided at small clinics, and mobile clinics were organized twice a week by Grameen health assistants in their own villages. The mobile clinics provided basic check-ups, including weight and blood pressure, while simple preventative care was provided at the household level. Some care was delivered through mobile phones. A common TV advertisement promoted 24-hour access to doctors for a fifteen taka per minute fee, but illiteracy and the high cost of the service prevented many villagers from utilizing the service.

The ethnographic studies provided a rich tapestry of village life and allowed Kazi and Narayan to tease out all the threads that affected healthcare access: household incomes, individual mindsets, literacy and education, locations and methods, services, and efficacy. As Kazi put it,

> Often, we try to find a quick answer to a problem we are trying to solve. But this [study was] more about taking the time to put yourself in the village. What would life be like? It should describe the people, the

culture and the community. We should not expect ethnography studies to give you the answer. But [they are] a good way to get down to the grass-roots level. We realized we need to impact a small community first in a meaningful way on its own terms. Success there would lead us to replicate it across other communities.

By using data to construct a complete picture of village life, they were able to identify gaps that a technology intervention could fill. It was clear that mobile phones were widely used, that remittance earnings had a multiplier effect on the local economy and gave families more spending power, that high rates of illiteracy affected villagers' ability to proactively seek or utilize healthcare solutions, and that existing healthcare assistants had effective reach in local communities. They now had a baseline from which they could explore different possibilities.

Technology Design Improvements

Based on these findings, Grameen Intel began work on a healthcare programme that built on the initial pilot project and kept maternal health as a focus. This would be a new-packaged software, *shumātā*, targeted to help pregnant women. The concept combined the idea of remote access by doctors with in-person visits by trained mobile nurses, utilizing the best aspects of each while avoiding some of the pitfalls of a call centre. The *shumātā* software could be installed on smartphones used by healthcare workers in the field, and provided a set of simple tools to screen pregnant women for risk factors such as age, number of past pregnancies, length of time since their last medical check-up, previous C-sections, stillbirths and other issues. Information collected in this way was sent wirelessly to the relevant clinic, where a doctor would provide immediate analysis and feedback remotely. Pregnant women identified as high-risk could then be referred for follow-up care at a village clinic or city healthcare facility, depending on their needs.

Kazi and Narayan needed to quickly get up to speed on software product design beyond the prototype they had developed earlier. They found a software application developed by social enterprise Dimagi, an outgrowth of MIT's Media Lab, that had a similar electronic record-keeping system. This would potentially enable them to jump-start the design process by using an existing technology that could be localized and leveraged for new applications. Yunus had earlier discussed how existing electronic records were complicated and had too many bells and whistles, which was overkill for a village clinic: information for the sake of information was not what the villagers were looking for or needed. Instead, it had to provide pertinent information around a specific condition, some basic analytics, and a tangible result or action. Not tons of data, but suggestions that a nurse could use after a few clicks.

Narayan travelled to Massachusetts to meet Jonathan Jackson, CEO of Dimagi, a start-up focused on the use of technology for underserved communities around the world. They had ongoing projects in Africa working with various development agencies and NGOs. What caught Narayan's attention was Dimagi's focus on front-line workers and the use of existing infrastructure—their technology would work on a current phone network with smartphones. Their technologies included data collection and monitoring by mobile nurses who would make home visits to their patients.

On the outskirts of Cambridge, Narayan found the nondescript building that Dimagi considered their home. Jonathan was soft-spoken, and with his long hair, T-shirt, jeans and sneakers reflected the stereotypical software engineer. His company, at this point, had less than ten employees, mostly recent MIT graduates, but they had a long-term vision of the potential of technology for the underserved. When Jonathan walked Narayan through their approach and existing software, it became apparent that their technology was geared towards implementation in local environments where Grameen Intel operated. It could be further refined based on Grameen Intel's focus area of maternal health, which was ideal. They agreed on a short-term project where Grameen Intel would come up with a software that was solely focused on the key problems they had identified. It had a simpler interface, a shorter list of data, and a simple report that produced actionable recommendations.

In a few months, Grameen Intel's collaboration with Dimagi gave them something more usable, a simple electronic records solution specific to maternal care. However, on the implementation side, dealing with nurses continued to create unexpected challenges. They realized that while nurses had vocational training, it was not at the level of literacy that would be expected in the

West. They had to simplify the verbiage and encourage doctors to teach the nurses more of the context behind each of the database fields.

When dealing with low literacy, as they learnt from their previous prototype, Kazi and Narayan realized they needed to turn the steps into a simple process, like an assembly line. The software provided a way to standardize the questions a nurse would ask patients at various visits. It had to be simple, clear and laid out in step-by-step fashion like a software algorithm or a decision tree. It had to be bulletproof from the standpoint of reducing the judgement and skills required. Standardizing the process was critical for effective healthcare delivery at the base of the pyramid, but getting to those simple steps was not easy.

Once the new software was developed and tested, it was still unclear if the business model would work. Initially, *shumātā* was launched in four clinics, each with a doctor and six nurses. Each clinic served a five-kilometre radius which had, at any given time, about 800 pregnant women. The clinics offered a service package of 200 taka per year (about $2.50), which entitled clients to multiple nurse visits and a member's rate of twenty taka for a doctor's visit, versus a non-member rate of forty taka. Their research had shown that more than half of the women eligible for membership would, at various phases of their pregnancies, be categorized as high-risk based on World Health Organization guidelines.

Kazi and Narayan believed that a technology-based business model would increase their footprint and bring in more revenue for the clinics. If they could increase the number of members signed up for the service package by 200 to 300, they would be making strides. The antenatal-care package would be enabled by technology. Mobile devices carried by the nurses would capture relevant data and log them in the back-end for doctors to view and highlight areas of risk or follow-ups required for the mother. Standardized information would be delivered to the mother about her necessary intake of vitamins, minerals, and folic acid. That was the version of the business model and social impact they had on paper.

They had all the support from the headquarters-level management teams who administered the local clinics, but local uptake continued to be a struggle even with more effective technology based on learning from the field. Nurses were reluctant to take on learning and using a new system, when they felt comfortable with their existing paper-based processes. As Ishrak had warned, developing proper incentive structures for front-line workers, doctors and clinic administrators also became a major issue. Nurses were paid 4,000 taka each month and doctors 15,000 taka simply to show up at work. Additional revenue enabled by technology did not help their bottom line because there was no business manager or commission-based employees. Attrition among doctors was high because of their reluctance to work in rural areas, further complicating the model.

Even in the second phase, Grameen Intel struggled to financially link all parties in the value chain, limiting their ability to deploy the technology at scale, despite the improved technology effectiveness of *shumātā*. This time, a more thoughtful, human-centred process of research and design had enabled the creation of a solution, but the larger systemic failings of the public healthcare system continued to be a limitation. Still, they had a prototype that worked because of its simplicity—a simplicity not borne from the quick search for a solution but from the long time spent on interviews, personal experience and expert research. Simple was not the same as easy, as Kazi was discovering:

> What we realized is even when you are trying to make social impact, business drivers remained critical. The technology was working, but the system was more complex. There are issues with incentives that needed to be worked out. Without them, a financially sustainable business model is just a cliché.

After two rounds of learnings, Kazi and Narayan continued to move forward with the belief that steady progress can gradually overcome most challenges. Although they liked to think in terms of 'bits and bytes', they realized that they were at the mercy of entrenched players who were used to a different system. Their version of simplicity in this round was still not simple enough for stakeholders to adopt. There was not enough clarity on the value delivered at the personal level for all involved. Kazi and Narayan would eventually make another attempt with one simple health and wellness device based on one simple business model.

Key Lessons:

- Find a specific, focused solution; these are more likely to generate real impact and scale quickly.
- 'Peel the onion': ask questions and reveal the layers involved in a vertically integrated solution to a common problem.
- 'Don't boil the ocean': understand and accept your limitations as a start-up social business, even if seeking larger scale in the long term.

SIX

Simplicity Is Complex

It's easy to design a device or system that is complex but much harder to take something complicated and boil it down to its essence. While Grameen Intel struggled to move the healthcare application *shumātā* out of the earlier stages of intrapreneurship, the soil-testing software *mrittikā* had established (by design) an aspect of virality that enabled users to easily share their experience with others and provided a springboard to better revenue generation. A major part of this success was due to the ease of use of the technology and delivery model, refined through empathy for the users that came from in-depth ethnographic research and personal interaction.

The ability to make a solution usable and actionable strongly rests on packaging the solution into smaller bits that address specific, meaningful problem points. As Kazi put it, 'Simplicity is not simple; on the contrary, it requires hiding inherent complexity. Solutions that are put forward should not be more complex than the problems they are designed to solve.' The interaction between a user and a device needs to be simple. Think of a phone where typing in a few digits connects you to another person. Or, think of the apps on an iPhone, which typically have a single function each: a map that shows you the best way to get to a destination, or a weather forecast for your weekend. But when it comes to a business model derived from a technology device, the business model itself also needs to have the same elegant simplicity.

For example, even today in Bangladesh, there are people who provide a service to the local population by helping them fill out various types of forms (applying for birth certificates, land lease applications, etc.), using none other than a traditional typewriter. In this scenario, the typewriter is the technology solution, and the business model is what the typist would charge based on the type or length of the form being completed. The entrepreneur typically recoups the cost of the typewriter in a few months. Similarly, we are working towards identifying the twenty-first-century version of these business models targeted towards individuals, thus creating a source of livelihood enabled by technology that they would not have otherwise.

Enabling better livelihoods is a key element in reducing worldwide poverty, which can benefit from the same mindset. The complexity of conditions driving poverty is enormous, whether related to agricultural productivity, healthcare access or quality education. These problems can't be solved single-handedly, or by a single organization, despite the enormous effort put into analysis and discussion through governments, the UN, the World Economic Forum and other actors. The key, in Kazi's words, 'is someone taking the first step to come up with a solution that will work in a market setting, and that is simple enough from both technology and business delivery standpoint to be used'.

To facilitate market adoption (or 'virality' in Yoskovitz and Croll's framework) among the poor, a solution has to be simply explained. When Grameen Intel introduced their soil-testing software, Kazi and Narayan explained it from a technical standpoint, true to their technical backgrounds. They began with a discussion of soil macronutrients, their effects on plant growth, and how to effectively analyse and supplement the balance of each, expecting quick uptake once farmers understood the benefits. Perhaps unsurprisingly, uptake was not quite as fast as expected.

As Kazi dug into the problem, he came away with a belief that at a more fundamental level, technical information is only valuable to someone who, true to the word, is able to value it, i.e. someone with a formal education. It was difficult, at first, to understand the mindset of someone who didn't even know how to read or write—to experience the empathy at the root of effective social innovation. The farmers they sought to help practised farming in ways handed down through generations. A farmer trusted his or her parents, who showed them what to do, because it worked. How could Grameen Intel explain that 'yields were suboptimal'? They could try explaining it in words but couldn't point out the problem instantly. Their descriptions of data and trends were met with a blank look. Kazi learnt that the key decision-making criterion for most farmers was one of trust. If you established trust first, they had faith in the information you presented. The most effective way to bring the concept and reality together was in terms of a real story.

This was the challenge they faced irrespective of how effective the technology solution was. They needed to find a trusted spokesperson who could tell a story. There wasn't much in the way of superstars in rural Bangladeshi agriculture to draw from, so a celebrity endorsement wasn't going to work. But they thought that a more honest story, and a more effective one, could come from one of the farmers. They needed a lead farmer who had tried the solution and could share his or her experience, someone who could be the human face of the software. This person could show how the software helped analysis of soil conditions and showed how to improve crop yields, thereby increasing farmer incomes. The role of a human intermediary was critical.

Grameen Intel's field team began identifying one or two lead farmers in each village where they were operating. The idea was simple: farmers would allocate a portion of their land where they implemented the software's recommendation, and they would farm the rest in the traditional way to see if there was a difference. The effort was called 'Project Harvest'. This was designed to build off the initial test results in India, where a few farmers who had used the technology saw their fertilizer costs decrease due to more precise application and also saw their yields increase—a counter-intuitive result that contradicted the 'more is better' approach advocated by many agricultural input companies. The results had then been compared with other farmers in the same area who were growing the same crops but did not use the computerized recommendations.

Every time Grameen Intel did this experiment, the results were in their favour. After that, it was easy to ask these farmers and others if they wanted to try the software on their entire plot. They didn't have to rely on Grameen Intel's advice—they could see the results for themselves. They could talk to someone in their community who had benefited from it. Grameen Intel's field agents were no longer there to give a lecture on the use of technology, different types of soil macronutrients, and the roles of key stakeholders in agricultural value chains. They were only there to tell farmers what someone in their own village had done: 'It's more yields and increased income. It's simply a clever thing to do.'

Kazi and Narayan's top lesson after months of effort was to focus on one thing that could move the needle, in their case testing for macronutrients in the soil. The next lesson was to make the message as clear as possible, by helping potential customers talk to a farmer who had done it and see for themselves if it was 'clever' and the right thing to do. They had to be brief and to the point in terms of how they conveyed the message. This could become a theoretical exercise when working with marginal farmers who owned only a small piece of land. Instead, it was all about increasing their income and providing a simple path to get there.

To make things even more challenging, Grameen Intel had to distinguish the end user of the service from the ultimate beneficiary. In this case, the beneficiary was the farmer, but the end user was the service provider who actually utilized the software. This user might be a government extension officer, an entrepreneur serving multiple farmers, or the farmer himself/herself. Like many businesses, even within this group of end users, Grameen Intel had multiple customer types, each with different value propositions that appealed to them, sales channels through which they could be reached, and preferred types of relationships.

The Soil Doctor

Kazi and Narayan tried to establish working relationships with government extension officers in Bangladesh and India to spread the technology but found it difficult to break through barriers caused by their incentives and motivations. In Bangladesh, they went to the Ministry of Agriculture to determine the best sales channel, but nobody could tell them whom to talk to about the technology in the first place. Then they referred Kazi to the Ministry of Posts, Telecommunications and Information Technology, which asked in turn if the solution had been certified by the Ministry of Agriculture. At the grass-roots level, local extension officers were not interested in discussing the technology without permission from the central office. So, the Ministry of Agriculture was responsible for approving the technology, but nobody at the ministry knew who to speak with to secure that approval.

Interacting directly with entrepreneurs who would serve multiple farmers was a more promising possibility. They found several NGOs already working with farmers on improving agricultural output, typically through programmes funded by external grants. Grameen Intel partnered with Solidaridad Network Asia to devise a field test that would compare different fertilizer application practices to determine the optimum, result-driven recommendation service. Solidaridad already had multiple projects in the region with a specific focus on improving agricultural output while utilizing fewer resources, and on improving prices paid to farmers by buying or selling as a group.

The collaboration focused on two regions over a period of two seasons, where Solidaridad selected a number of individuals who could provide soil-testing services in their local community. The potential entrepreneurs were provided with step-by-step software training to analyse the soil, determine fertilizer requirements and advise on seed purchases. This capacity-building project focused on long-term financial sustainability with the entrepreneurs continuing to provide these services and the farmers embedding soil testing in their regular agricultural practices. Grameen Intel was able to later develop and expand these partnerships through a range of other NGOs, including Helvetas, Practical Action and iDE, among others.

Working directly with farmers proved to be more of a stretch, at least in South Asia. Most farmers did not have the education necessary to operate a computer or smartphone, so any recommendations around optimal fertilizer and nutrient application had to be very direct, i.e. 'this is how you do it' versus 'here's a printout of what you need'. This meant that, by default, the primary end user ended up becoming the intermediary service provider—local entrepreneurs working in a small area and trained by partner NGOs.

The person they had to keep in mind when designing the software interface was therefore not the farmer but the entrepreneur providing the service who would act as the local 'soil doctor'. Soil conditions varied from season to season, and fertilizer recommendations would also vary depending on the crop, so multiple soil tests might be needed in any given year for a single farmer. So there was a strong potential for ongoing, repeated demand, provided the farmers saw the value of the service the 'soil doctor' was providing. In order to enable the service, the software recommendations needed to be provided as a set of very specific, actionable steps that the entrepreneur could then easily communicate to the beneficiary.

The initial version of the software provided recommendations in kilograms per hectare, applied in one-, three- or six-month intervals. While that information was important, Grameen Intel had to go beyond that to simply say, for example, 'one month from now you will have to add . . .' They began to think of the recommendations like the script of a simple play to be acted out by the intermediary for the benefit of the farmer. Even the exact words and phrases used were important. It also needed to be consistent and repeatable, since the skill and education level of the entrepreneur could vary widely.

Fortunately, software is a fantastic enabler for making things consistent and repeatable. Creating a process where all entrepreneurs offered a similar recommendation in the same manner, in a way that could be easily understood by farmers, created the capacity to scale. They were able to quickly replicate the training for entrepreneurs, turning it into a science.

With the pilot results showing good social impact, IFAD (the UN's International Fund for Agricultural Development) reached out to Grameen Intel to see if there would be interest in expanding to Cambodia, where the government had a goal of becoming the largest rice exporter in the world. This was a tremendous opportunity for Grameen Intel and the team jumped on it to test their solutions at a national scale working with the Ministry of Agriculture of the Government of Cambodia, IDE and a couple of local implementation agencies on a nation-wide pilot with IDE to train a group of 230 service providers using tablets with the software pre-loaded. This contract, Grameen Intel's first big revenue, was booked by the company's new business development manager, Dilek Altin.

Of course, none of that would have been possible had they not transitioned from a software interface that produced a recommendation using technical data to a recommendation using easily understood messages. Any organization working at the base of the pyramid using technology needs to put more focus on the 'easy to understand' and 'easy to follow up on' portion of the interface. It needs to be interesting. It needs to resonate. Otherwise, even the most complex algorithm and thousands of lines of supporting code will have no value to the population segment one is trying to impact.

gSlate

One way to provide digital information in a simple format is the practice of skeuomorphism, or design that mimics a physical predecessor. The metaphors of the 'desktop' and 'folder' in computing are a few ubiquitous examples. This proved to be a useful paradigm for Grameen Intel when they first entered the realm of education. Seeking to provide an educational software tool that would benefit young children, they created gSlate, a reading and writing app designed to look like the slate chalkboards common in Bangladesh. Users are presented with numbers or letters that they can trace, complete with the sound of chalk, and hear them pronounced in English or their native language. The app is designed for tablets using the Android operating system, more common than Apple's iOS in developing nations, and made available for free to educators on Google's online store.

gSlate was intended to boost early language development skills and provide a gentle introduction to using digital devices, an increasingly important skill for work and education. In the US and Europe, parents may lament the effects of digital technology on their children, but in developing nations it can make a critical difference in career readiness. Think of the number of jobs and degrees that require some form of digital literacy, and now extrapolate that out by fifteen years, to when gSlate users will be entering the workforce or attending college. A simple, well-designed application could thus have huge impacts on the earning potential of the next generation.

The Magic Bangle

For adults who had never been exposed to digital technologies, however, more creative approaches to conveying information were needed. Grameen Intel made another leap in what they meant by an 'interface' as they designed their next health solution. Like *shumātā*, the target was to improve maternal wellness, but the problem addressed was not an intuitive link—it was smoke. According to the World Health Organization, nearly three billion people worldwide cook indoors over an open fire or traditional stove (2016). These can create high levels of carbon monoxide (CO) and particulate matter, which are especially dangerous to pregnant women or small children, who also happen to be those members of the family that spend the most time indoors. Household air pollution kills an estimated 4.3 million people each year (World Health Organization, 2016), more than tuberculosis, malaria and HIV combined (Murray, 2014).

A robust global marketplace for lower-polluting, inexpensive 'rocket stoves' had arisen, but the scale of the need far outstripped the market, and even those new stoves produced some CO. Kazi and Narayan determined that a warning device was needed that could alert families to dangerous CO levels so that they could open windows and doors or move outside. It had to be very cheap and always present when needed, which meant that a wearable personal device could be the best option. Unlike wearable health devices in the West, however, where customers are accustomed to such technology, it had to be both very simple to use and appealing for everyday wear.

Throughout South Asia, women wear decorative bangles on their ankles and wrists. Making the device a bangle meant that it would be worn by the group they were most hoping to reach, would always be in the same space as the woman, and wouldn't require any changes in behaviour. The device, called a Carbon Monoxide Exposure Limiter, (COEL), had a speaker but no screen, to not only conserve batteries but also to make its use and interaction more simple and suitable for a target segment who were largely unable to read. Instead, when a CO monitor in the bangle detects dangerous levels of the gas, it flashes a red warning light and plays a recorded message in the language of the listener encouraging them to open windows and doors or move outside. It can also play more than eighty maternal health reminders. Made of colourful, moulded plastic, the device is water-resistant and has a ten-month battery life (no need to plug it in on your bedside table every night) (Kirsch). COEL was priced at roughly $15–20 if produced in large volumes to ensure affordability for users and financial sustainability for Grameen Intel.

The idea for COEL came from a chance meeting Narayan had with Lakshman Krishnamurthy, an Intel Fellow who was then leading the Applied Innovation Engineering team. Lakshman's team was looking at technologies and case studies for wearable environmental sensors, with particular emphasis on outdoor air pollution. These were sensors that could detect relevant amounts of carbon monoxide, sulfur oxides and nitrogen oxides, which are key air pollutants. The project was named 'Canary', after the proverbial 'canary in a coal mine' used to alert miners of air pollution. Continuing the metaphor, the koel is a type of bird native to South Asia.

Kazi and Narayan latched on to the possibility of detecting harmful amounts of indoor air pollution using these sensors. However, the technology needed to be translated into a form-factor device that was not only functional but that women would want to own and wear. Working with Lakshman's broader team, they created a requirements document that detailed items such as the bangle's shape and dimensions, a battery life exceeding ten months (longer than pregnancy), a sensor small enough and sensitive enough to function effectively in the device, and an appealing design. Lakshman's brilliant team of engineers, within a matter of months, came back with a set of prototypes that satisfied and checked all the technical requirements. But perhaps unsurprisingly, their team of Western engineers struggled to create a jewellery device that would be desirable for rural women in South Asia. Narayan ended up bringing in an industrial design firm from Chennai, India, who had not only worked on smart wearables, but also understood local jewellery and design elements.

Once the industrial design was complete and the prototype devices built, Kazi and Narayan needed to understand if COEL would work in the actual environment it was meant for. They worked with Cindy Merrill, a thorough and extremely methodical User Interaction Engineer in Intel's User Experience and

Interactive Design group to design field trials in India, Nepal and Bangladesh that would explore wearability, usability, aesthetics and functionality. The device had to be comfortable to wear, communicate warnings that were easy to understand, function in extreme conditions of heat and humidity, and be desirable in a social context. All of this development and iteration required a budget and a truly supportive executive sponsor who believes in the basic tenet that technology needs to drive social impact and they found it in Lakshman's manager, Steve Holmes, who was the Vice President and leading the Smart Devices Innovation team at Intel.

The field trials were extremely critical in truly understanding whether the device would 'work' in the context and the environment it was designed for. They also revealed unexpected findings that we would never have realized if not for the field trials. One unexpected feedback and learning was that early testers in one village were afraid that the bangle contained a camera that would record them because of the presence of coloured LEDs. To address this concern, the design was changed to eliminate multiple LEDs on the bangle and the number of times it would light up which also helped in conserving battery life. On the positive side, there was the clear sense of ownership and a status symbol in wearing the 'magic' bangle. Other feedback mentioned that the bangle was bulky compared to what was typically worn; could get in the way when doing chores; the volume for warning messages was not sufficiently loud; and that dust accumulated around the tiny speakers.

The feedback from these tests helped inform the final design, which still had to overcome major technical challenges. Mourad Souag, lead engineer in the project, described the barriers they overcame:

The first of these challenges was to design a device that would not require recharging during long months of usage in rural areas. To make it work, every microwatt of power consumption had to be carefully considered and managed. All the components that go into the electronics of the bangle had to be selected based on energy efficiency. Physical challenges included finding a battery that fit the curved bangle shape and would last 10 months on a single charge in the high temperatures of India. Imagine a smartwatch that would last ten months on a single charge! Extensive research on battery technology allowed us to identify what we were looking for. Most of the batteries in the market were done using a winding process. Those are easier to make because it doesn't cost as much in tools and can run quick on the line. Talking to a battery expert at Intel, we understood that a better process is to stack layers of the battery instead of winding.

The other key challenge we worked on was to have multiple designs of the bangle available to the customer, while still keeping the costs of manufacturing manageable. This balance let us use the more cost-effective option of plastic injection moulding, which was more durable and allowed for multiple colour options. To enable different design aesthetics, we had colourful designs printed on to a PSA polymer film and applied to the surface. This allowed for a plethora of colours and designs that could be manufactured.

The sensor used for detecting the smoke was also a challenge. A small and cheap sensor was available and would be easy to integrate; unfortunately, this sensor would use too much energy, shortening the battery life of the product to only one month. We had to select a more power-efficient design. But this sensor was ten times more expensive, increasing the product cost by 25 per cent. It was a delicate dance with the sensor company to make them see the potentially huge opportunity as well as social impact that their sensors would have. The way that happened was when we made the first set of prototypes to prove the feasibility and convince them that it would be possible to make such a wearable, small form-factor device.

While the technical challenges were addressed by the engineers at Intel, shepherding the manufacturing was largely done by the Grameen Intel engineers led by Razib who spent weeks at the factory working with the contract manufacturer on issues ranging from picking the right kind of glue, to assembling the bangle so that it does not trigger the sensitive sensor inside, to picking the right combination and distribution of housing colors and the sticker design covering the bangle that is culturally appropriate for the deployments. The mechanical and functional part of the solution was one thing, but the health proposition for a typical customer was another challenge, even if they could produce a device that met user criteria. Carbon monoxide is odourless, so they were asking a villager to purchase something that would protect them from something that they could not see or smell. How do you explain that to someone whom you think has a need but will not value it and therefore will not demand it? This is a common dilemma when working in low-income areas, trying to convince someone to part with money that they already don't have enough of. Should the money not be spent on higher priorities like food and shelter?

On the device side, drawing on the strength of Intel's internal resources, as well as external partnerships, enabled the Grameen Intel team to overcome technical challenges that might be insurmountable for an independent entrepreneur. In this way, they benefited from an intrapreneurial approach that, in the words of Gifford Pinchot, enabled the 'independence of the entrepreneur while still holding over them the technological, financial, and perhaps most significant, the informational umbrella of the corporation' (1978).

That informational umbrella helped Kazi and Narayan realize their belief that they needed to move away from a general computing device. The new paradigm of a single-purpose device had all the elements of what they had learnt as they designed their earlier products: it needed to go after a specific problem, have a simple usage model, and be embedded in the users' daily lives. Serving a population segment with little education, they had to force themselves to think of a world where a computing device did not have a keyboard and a monitor that displayed 'reams and reams of information hoping something will stick' with the user, as Kazi put it.

The new wearable device was a perfect example of a natural interface and actionable information—the right information at the right time.

Key Lessons:

- Ease of use is critical, whether in the technology deployed or the usage model.
- It's important to package complex solutions into simple, easy-to-use products.
- Counter-intuitively, a high level of technical expertise is often required to make things simple.

SEVEN

Create Income, Not Consumption

More than half of the people in the world don't have a formal job. Official statistics show a global unemployment rate of close to six per cent—nearly 200 million people—but the actual numbers are almost certainly higher, especially in developing nations with incomplete data. Even among those who are employed, nearly fifty per cent of non-agricultural workers participate in the informal economy, which offers low pay with few protections (International Labour Organization, 2016). But jobs are essential to improving health and education outcomes because having an income makes everything else more affordable. One of the world's most pressing problems, then, is unemployment.

Take the analogy of a taxi driver who receives an upfront loan to purchase a taxi. He provides a service that generates an income, which enables him to make monthly payments, and any surplus becomes his livelihood. But what if you replaced that taxi with a computing device? What kind of service would he be able to provide? Would that computing device give him a tool for income generation? Grameen Intel's soil-testing software, *mrittikā*, was an experiment in that direction. The entrepreneurs providing that service had to think like a business person and so did the managers of Grameen Intel, despite pursuing a social mission: How many customers were needed to break even? How could they market their services? Kazi and Narayan wanted to make a difference in the areas of agriculture, healthcare and education using technology. But like the taxi driver, the investment one makes in a computing device needed to be capitalized to generate income.

In one of the villages they visited, there was a small shop for passport pictures. The owner was a twenty-something unemployed youth who owned a digital camera and a photo printer connected to a laptop. The Grameen Intel team wanted to come up with creative uses of technology that could help create such small-scale businesses and support similarly creative entrepreneurs. As Kazi put it,

Most of those who work in the corporate world are driven by Wall Street's expectations of top-line growth, new market entry, and competitive differentiation. When a company already has an installed customer base, this approach and these kinds of metrics make sense. How else would you measure your business performance? When businesses think of the population at the 'base of the pyramid', they

quickly apply the same set of measures. How can a
solution penetrate this population segment to drive the
top line? In the long run, the actions will eventually
lead to revenue growth and economic prosperity for
all, but in the short term, steps to get there are very
different.

Most corporate executives focus on the total available
market (the number of customers they could reach
under perfect conditions), market segment (which
customers they want to reach) and market share (how
many of those potential customers they actually reach).
When companies have well-to-do customers and seek to
extract a share of their disposable income, this approach
makes sense and works well. If a customer plans to
spend $1,000 on a computer or smartphone, then there
are various ways to influence how those dollars can
flow to a certain firm or product. Advertisements, brand
promotions and customer engagement are all meant to
do precisely that.

However, taking this formula and applying it to the
four billion people without much disposable income
raises a number of issues, from financial to moral.
Creating more consumers—expanding the total available
market—means creating more jobs. Corporations have
generated millions of jobs across the world in product
development, and high-tech companies in India and
China alone have done so on a massive scale, but
formal-sector employment only reaches a fraction
of the population. Selling a product or service that,
in turn, enables consumers to become entrepreneurs

can positively influence income generation, poverty alleviation and market growth.

The transportation industry, for example, can have a huge impact on a country's GDP. What is often overlooked are the entrepreneurial opportunities that the car industry has produced. General Motors (GM) can claim millions of jobs created from design to production, but how many entrepreneurs like that taxi driver has GM indirectly created around the world? This structure is now beginning to play out in the world of computing. As just one example, eBay enables anyone to operate as an entrepreneur through a computing platform where products are bought and sold. In the process, the entrepreneur becomes both a service provider and a consumer. But software, unlike cars, offers a much easier way to support entrepreneurship among groups in poverty.

Entrepreneurship among the global poor can be an expression of self-determination and creativity, but more often than not, it is a simple necessity. In countries with limited employment opportunities, especially for individuals without much education, entrepreneurship may be the only option for many. Abhijit Banerjee and Esther Duflo estimate that nearly twenty-four per cent of the extremely poor (earning less than $0.99 per day) who live in rural areas run a non-agricultural business, a number that rises to forty-four per cent in cities (2011). In their book *Poor Economics,* they state that 'there are more than a billion people who run their own farm or business.' Whether or not entrepreneurship is their first choice, expanding income-generation opportunities for these individuals—especially if done in a way that respects their dignity and provides additional benefits for their communities—is an essential step in reducing global poverty.

Creating a Small-Business Owner

When Grameen Intel was formed, it was clear the company could not succeed on a financial or social level if it viewed customers solely as consumers. The approach could not just be identifying ways for them to purchase more devices. Their disposable income was needed for food, water, healthcare and education, not software. The mission of Grameen Intel was to create products that helped people become entrepreneurs, as though GM had a division aimed at making more taxi drivers. Creating an entrepreneurial class at the base of the pyramid that uses a company's product as an income-generation tool has a spillover effect of more consumption. Many corporations attempting to secure market share from this segment try to reach the consumption part too quickly; it may take a generation or two to create sizeable impact. To reach the base of the pyramid, job creation needs to come first.

In some ways, this is a return to the fundamental concept of how a village-based economy might form. First is the farmer, then maybe a village doctor or healer, then the cobbler or other service providers and merchants. We forget that the farmer, doctor and cobbler are all entrepreneurs. Today, many Fortune 500 companies were created by one or two individuals who started as an entrepreneur. Communities and economies are created because of entrepreneurship, and the formula isn't any different when looking at the base of the pyramid. Who will be the next version of the farmer or the cobbler? How can they access technology that gives them more opportunities to be entrepreneurs?

In one of Kazi and Narayan's first meetings with Muhammad Yunus, he told them the story of the 'cell phone ladies'. In 1997, mobile phones were rare and largely unaffordable for most of the population in Bangladesh, but there was a clear need. Many villagers had relatives living in larger cities, and at the time their only means of communication was by mail. As cell phones became more available, Grameen Bank saw an opportunity to facilitate connections between distant family members and create entrepreneurs using the technology, while building on the bank's existing services and networks. Grameen Bank would identify borrowers who could take a loan to purchase a phone. These borrowers would then sell use of the phone to their neighbours for the cost of airtime plus a profit margin. They became, in effect, a walking phone booth.

At the programme's peak, there were more than 280,000 cell phone ladies who purchased both phones and airtime from Grameenphone, a for-profit joint venture between Grameen Telecom and Telenor (Shaffer, 2007). A cell phone lady would take a loan to purchase a phone along with prepaid minutes. Soon after, word would spread about the presence of a phone in the village, and villagers would immediately see an opportunity to talk to their friends and relatives living in cities or working abroad. They would become customers of the phone lady, who would let them use the phone and in turn would collect money based on the cost per minute of their calls plus a profit margin. Buying a cell phone and selling airtime became a profitable business. It also became a shared resource for the community that they could all benefit from.

Over time, the rapid spread of cheap cell phones expanded the benefits of phone ownership. Separate studies have found that for every ten per cent increase in cell phone usage in countries like Bangladesh, GDP grows by more than half a per cent (Foster, 2007). Grameenphone is now the largest mobile telecom provider in Bangladesh, and invested $1.2 billion in communications infrastructure that helped make cell phones ubiquitous in the country (Grameenphone, 2016). Although the phone-lady concept was invaluable to demonstrate the value of technology and telecommunications in their start-up phase, the benefit to society as a whole over time was inarguably larger.

Agriculture was ripe for a similar approach. In Bangladesh, the agriculture sector contributes about fourteen per cent of total GDP and employs forty-one per cent of the labour force (FAO). Depletion of soil organic matter through intensive agriculture and overuse of fertilizers had caused deterioration of the soil, and along with the lack of access to agriculture information and expertise, limited the income of the farmers. Getting appropriate information at the level of individual fields was an opportunity to reverse the trend.

Grameen Intel's eAgro sought to create a similar business for their clients, who would provide services to their community enabled by a computing device but wouldn't tether it to a specific piece of hardware. Instead, they would develop and deploy a software application that could be stored and distributed online, easily updated, and used on a range of devices. Cell phones are now widespread and smartphones are becoming increasingly common so the first suggestion from a Western tech firm is usually 'build an app'. But when millions of farmers lack even basic literacy, a smartphone app may not be an option. How about a central help desk with specialized software that a farmer can call for support? First, there would have to be enough eAgro experts to sit in these call centres, and second, they would have to dispatch a 'technician' to take soil samples for testing, an approach with high overhead expenses. Clearly, that business model wouldn't work for Grameen Intel.

Instead, they took farmer needs for additional income-generating opportunities (the 'hear' phase of Human-Centred Design), brainstormed promising approaches and selected effective elements of other solutions ('create'), and applied practical considerations for financial sustainability and scalability ('deliver') to settle on a soil-testing entrepreneur, very much like the cell phone lady. This alleviated the need for every farmer to have a smartphone or tablet. The entrepreneur, carrying a briefcase of test tubes and chemicals and a computing device with a software application, would offer a service to the local farmers: take a sample, do a test.

As described earlier, the process had two steps. First, the entrepreneur took a soil sample, put it in a test tube, and applied chemicals to check macronutrient levels. Then, they recorded the resulting reagent colours in a software application. The app quickly provided a recommendation on how much and what type of fertilizer to apply for the specific crop the farmer was trying to grow, and provided the time interval of what had to be added and when during the crop cycle. Other applications recommended seed types, input sellers and additional useful information.

This model bypassed the issue of farmer illiteracy by only requiring the entrepreneurs to be able to read and write. It also reduced the fixed costs of the original concept, a call centre and dispatch system, which would have to be paid regardless of the level of demand. Instead, the entrepreneur made an upfront capital investment to purchase the lab kit, computing device and software for a total amount of $300–$400. The entrepreneurs then recouped their investment through soil-testing services they provided in a local area. The ideal price point for a soil-testing service is likely in the $1–$3 range to ensure affordability for local farmers. It then takes roughly 100–300 soil tests to recoup the cost of capital and begin generating a positive cash flow for ongoing services. An entrepreneur in Bangladesh would likely need to provide close to fifty soil tests each month, priced at $2 each, to earn a decent living.

Moin was one of the seventeen entrepreneurs who were trained soon after the first *mrittikā* software release and he reached out to almost 300 farmers. He was equipped with a laptop that enabled the provision of advisory services to local farmers. Moin acted as one of the local service providers to conduct soil tests and provide the computer-generated recommendations. For his first season, he provided soil testing to twenty-five farmers at 220 taka each, generating a total income of 5,000 taka, which was higher than his prior income. He had an education, but before this he only had temporary jobs that he was able to find intermittently. He saw an opportunity for more income, and for the upcoming season he wanted to double the number of farmer customers to fifty.

Prashant was another entrepreneur in Odisha, India, who was trained by Grameen Intel's business partner eKutir, a regional social enterprise. Prashant's income in some months peaked at Rs 20,000 (versus less than Rs 3,000 which he had earned earlier). A sizeable portion of the income in those specific months included commissions he earned through the sale of seeds and fertilizers in addition to selling the advisory service. He was also forming a farmer group that would meet regularly to talk about better farming practices and to share knowledge.

In a country with few employment opportunities, a local university graduate can return to his or her village and offer these services. This gives them the potential to create a real business, generate follow-on income opportunities for the farmers they serve, and ideally help increase food output, solving several problems at once. An elegant solution, if enough farmers could be convinced of the utility of the service, and if enough entrepreneurs could be created to serve that need.

Marketing

Successfully marketing the service was critical. Something going viral in social media wasn't going to work in Bangladesh where most farmers on the margins weren't exactly browsing the Web, posting on Facebook or using Twitter. Most likely, their only access to technology was a simple, 'dumb' cell phone. That meant marketing had to be old-fashioned as well: billboards, flyers, and the lead farmers who could set an example for their community. Grameen Intel didn't have much of a marketing budget, so instead they tried to 'plant the seed' for a model that could be replicated: the rule of one. They hoped that government agencies and global development organizations would take a winning concept and deploy it elsewhere. This required an entirely different form of marketing, one that could take the success stories of farmers and package them, along with compelling data, into a form that funding and implementing organizations valued. But the fundamental mission remained the same: reducing unemployment and underemployment among the poor.

An important part of this approach was to showcase one village that Grameen Intel called the 'Ideal Village'. The vision was to present a positive picture of a village where all the farmers were aware of the new agricultural services and were using the technology. The village selected had roughly 200 households, with seventy per cent or more engaged in farming and agriculture-related work. True to the rule of one, a single soil doctor was trained to use the computer and to generate fertilizer recommendations. Approximately 100 farmers were served for two crop cycles.

The marketing efforts included weekly farmer awareness meetings. Each meeting would start with a local folk song by a fellow farmer. The entrepreneur would then showcase examples of soil testing and impact on yields. Some of the meetings would also include local agents selling seeds and fertilizers to talk about their existing and new products that year. This would be followed by a discussion on the challenges faced by the farmers and a conversation to share knowledge.

To further build awareness, the campaign also included large posters, similar to the movie posters that we are all familiar with. The posters were displayed in high-traffic areas such as the weekly marketplace, which was broadly similar to the weekend farmers' markets in many small US towns. Given the tropical climate and heat in this part of the world, many of the sellers would sit under an umbrella with their produce laid out over a mat on the ground. Grameen Intel distributed a few umbrellas for free with a large product logo printed on them.

There was also a local salesperson—again just one— who would knock on doors and get to know people ('no solicitation' signs don't exist yet in Bangladesh). The salesperson would inquire about the well-being of the father, mother and children in the household and engage in other social discussions. They would end the conversation by giving a quick example of a lead farmer who had used the technology-enabled services and the value they derived from it. They would then leave behind a leaflet showing the face of a happy farmer with more details in the local language on how to request the service.

Not only did Grameen Intel promote the new soil-testing services in the village, they also promoted that village when they talked about the model in other villages. Their goal was that the ideal village would be a shining example to the rest of the country and other parts of the world. It reflected how technology could help create entrepreneurs and how it could impact the livelihood of farmers. If others saw the possibilities based on this example, they could imagine themselves in a similar state, and their village could be the next 'ideal village'. This was Grameen Intel's one marketing campaign. They had replicated it in two other villages and made the approach and various marketing materials available to NGO partners who were funding agriculture projects in other parts of the country. Whereas the technology was about starting with one farmer and one entrepreneur, the marketing approach was in essence about impacting one community at a time.

Key Lessons:

- Think of how your business solution can create jobs and income-generating opportunities, not just consumption.
- Clearly define your own business model, and that of your entrepreneurial clients.
- An entrepreneur is your best customer, because she is the person who ties together the problem, the solution and other customers.

EIGHT

Patient Capital, Patient Entrepreneurs

Any company, during its initial formation, requires upfront money to pay employees, rent office space and purchase equipment. In business terms, this is the company's 'start-up capital'. Because the company is at a stage when products still need to be developed, it isn't earning any sales revenue, and the entrepreneurs who started the business must find other ways to raise that initial capital. These funds can come from the founders themselves, other private individuals (such as 'friends, family and fools'), or venture capital firms that invest in various stages of a start-up. Any type of funder would typically receive an ownership stake in exchange for their investment, and if the company succeeds, the ownership percentage will have a monetary value. Facebook received its initial capital from the venture capitalist Peter Thiel in 2004; Google received funding from Ram Shriram in 1998; and for Amazon it was the parents of founder Jeff Bezos. WhatsApp received funding from the venture capital firm Sequoia Capital, and Alibaba was funded by SoftBank. For Grameen Intel, which would be launched as a stand-alone company, the idea was to secure funding from Intel Capital.

Although Craig Barrett and Muhammad Yunus had come to an understanding that forming a company was a good idea, it was up to Kazi to secure start-up funding from Intel Capital. Instead of an entrepreneur pitching his business idea to a venture capital company, this time it was an intrapreneur making a similar pitch to the internal corporate venture capital division. Like any large company, at Intel there were always multiple projects competing for funds, so a system had been established to prevent favouritism. Each idea had to be vetted to ensure it was in the interest of the shareholders and employees who ultimately had a stake in the success of the company. A committee of senior executives met regularly to hear presentations and make investment decisions.

Kazi was given a thirty-minute slot to talk about the proposal to create Grameen Intel and the funding it needed. He had to carefully think through the approach of justifying the investment, and he worked closely with Intel's investment manager for South Asia to develop the storyline. Yunus's work and his Nobel Peace Prize provided credibility, but the investment rationale had to tie back directly to Intel's goals. Most venture capital firms have a few key items they look for before they invest. For example, there needs to be a clearly identifiable market where the products being envisioned will be sold. Will that market grow over time? Who are the competitors, and how is your product different? Do you have the right talent? Do you have a management team who can execute the plan? Can progress be measured? Is the investment in line with their venture capital philosophy (since some firms may focus only in certain sectors, such as networking hardware or software as a service)? And finally, does this all make sense based on data, evidence, or other tangible observations?

Since the venture capital firm is putting their money at risk, taking a disciplined approach to their investment is necessary. Overall, the motivation is to generate a profit—the money they invest should give them a higher return than (let's say) the interest they would receive if the money was sitting idle in a bank account. Overall, the venture capital industry adds value to the economy by helping companies get off the ground, introducing new products, creating jobs, and often generating a lot of wealth for their shareholders. Not all investments succeed, but the idea is to have a few winners that can help offset losses on the investments that don't work out.

On 6 May 2008, Kazi walked into the meeting with Intel Capital to discuss Grameen Intel. The executives in the committee headed Intel divisions such as legal, treasury and Asia, and also included the President of Intel Capital. In his mind, Kazi was at a disadvantage walking into the meeting. This concept was not a good fit for what a venture capitalist typically funded. The first bullet on his first slide simply stated: 'Use information and communications technology (ICT) to bring the poor into the information society.' There were no data Kazi knew of that could help define the 'market segment'. When you think of people who live in poverty, that number is in the billions, but how does that rationalize a proposed investment? Nor did he have a differentiated set of products defined other than 'we will tackle telemedicine . . . provide access to quality medical care enabled by technology' as well as 'other solutions to benefit the impoverished segment'.

On the positive side, Intel Capital's investment philosophy saw value in bringing Intel's technology expertise to a segment of the population that did not currently benefit from technology. If Intel's processors could be used to take a rocket to the moon, why couldn't they be used to improve the lives of some of the most vulnerable people back here on Earth? That was the argument Kazi made in the meeting, without knowing which way the decision would land. Kazi also added that this was not going to be a charity but a real company—a social business that over time should recoup its operational costs, although seeking profits was not the primary purpose.

One of the executives present questioned whether there was sufficient talent available locally in Bangladesh. Kazi had done an initial calculation that showed there would be more than enough software engineers graduating from local universities to meet their relatively limited needs. These engineers would also be complemented by a leadership team that included managers from the US and India to help with set-up and training. If some of the products succeeded in Bangladesh, they could possibly look at Africa as a future growth opportunity.

There were lots of other tactical questions, such as tax status of the entity, the number of board members, and contract elements. This was mainly to understand the challenges of forming a company in Bangladesh, where Intel had very limited experience, and how Grameen could help fill those gaps. The more tangible data that Kazi did present was a detailed plan around the company set-up, possible solution areas (health, education), and preliminary metrics and goals around product milestones, solution adoption and financials.

Eventually, after thirty minutes of discussion, Kazi received an approval for initial funds. However, there was one more thing that Kazi wanted to clarify. Typically, in the venture capital industry, investments would have a very short timeline to assess the viability of the investment. This time period varies from deal to deal but often averages only three to five years. During this time, if the company finds that the fund invested in is on a positive trajectory, there may be additional investments to take the company to the next stage of expansion. However, if it's on a negative trajectory, the investors may just pull out. In the case of Grameen Intel, Kazi wanted to set the expectation that, given the level of uncertainty and the work they had to undertake, investors needed to be more patient before making an assessment as to whether the model was working. Grameen Intel needed not just venture capital, but 'patient capital'. At the end, the committee said 'yes, approved', but in Kazi's mind what they actually meant was 'okay, we're willing to make a first-ever investment in a purposeful social business'.

The venture capital industry often starts with the premise of investing money and knowledge with a goal of fast-tracking a business towards revenue growth, a public offering on a stock exchange, or perhaps an acquisition by a larger firm. Shareholders who own a certain percentage of the company make a profit in the process. However, the founders of Intel and Microsoft, for example, did not start with that mindset. They saw the potential of a new technology and were committed to building the product. They kept at it for multiple decades—once they had a workable solution, they kept working to take it to the next phase. Even now, their engineers are working on the next thing. During Kazi's meeting with the committee, he was able to steer the discussion towards using the investment for new technology uses and a population segment who could benefit from this work. They had to think beyond short-term financial gains or simple return on investment metrics and instead think of the long-term possibilities and how society could benefit.

Social entrepreneurs must have the same mindset when working on developing solutions for the base of the pyramid. They cannot be swayed by the dream of having a quick-success story. They need to build workable solutions and achieve small wins. Think of it as an experiment in progress. Start with winning one customer, then ten, and then the next thousand. Social entrepreneurs must understand how the solution fits the beneficiaries' lifestyle. Does it solve a real problem? Does it financially benefit him or her?

Along the way, you will have staff retention issues; there will be bureaucratic delays; approval for your export licences will not come through. You will learn that the local government is not incentivized to serve you and your company. Instead, they like ceremonial ribbon cuttings. But if you keep the big picture in mind, these will be minor hindrances. Roughly seventy per cent of the world is yet to benefit from information technology. Addressing that will mean taking on interesting challenges. Grameen Intel's drive for innovation will require the company to face new risks and uncertainties. Kazi and Narayan saw the business as 'a humble beginning, an experiment in progress, where the founders will continue to learn and innovate'.

Social businesses like Grameen Intel do not start with a product but a social impact objective. This was a key difference between their business and a high-tech start-up. Google, for example, had a product—a search engine—before it had a company. Most of these companies have a seed product as a starting point and use a company structure to serve customers. In Grameen Intel's case, there was no product, but they wanted to use technology to make a social impact. And they needed to identify how that could be done, which meant needing some leeway as they moved from concept to product. Traditional venture capitalists, on the other hand, are typically funding a company that already has a working prototype, a target customer segment, and would look for ways to serve that market as they seek higher revenues.

For Grameen Intel there were additional factors. Moving from concept to product added up to three years to Grameen Intel's start-up time frame. This involved research. For example, what does a typical household in a rural Indian village spend their discretionary money on? Then, they had to bring the right staff and partners on board, who understood the potential customers they were dealing with. It was a different type of work from the regular for-profit business world that they had previously understood and took for granted. This required that the start-up capital would need to cover the additional time and required more patience from the venture capital funders.

It took another eighteen months to get the company incorporated in Bangladesh. There were various different legal documents to navigate: company articles, shareholding contracts, share purchase agreements, etc. They needed to understand the local companies act and voting rights of various types of shares. They had to include clauses on the steps around company liquidation in case they ran out of money. This meant that developing product concepts and establishing the company took almost five years, definitely not what you would expect in the high-tech, venture capital world. Again, this took more time and money.

But that should be the expectation set from the beginning between those running the company and the shareholders and funders of the company. This needs to be part of the discussion between them and formalized as part of the business plan. For a social entrepreneur starting this type of business, there has to be an exploration timeline built into the overall financial model. In that scenario, one needs to determine that there is a core set of people spending a certain percentage of their time working towards key deliverables. They can come from various functional areas. You need to assign a project manager to identify the tasks, deliverables and timeline. This cannot be a casual project but one with real accountability.

For example, when Grameen Intel rolled out the eAgro soil-testing solution, they assigned a project manager who needed to submit a three-month plan with various tasks listed. When would they know which locations to cover? When would they train the local entrepreneurs providing the services? When would the computers be purchased? When would the software be set up? These are a few of the many tasks that the project manager would be accountable for. Then there were the metrics. How many farmers were they going to target? How many in the first month, and how many in the next? The project manager needed to be an employee of the Grameen Intel company, but at the same time, they also had a few Intel employees supporting the new venture. The managers of those employees needed to clearly indicate that it was not going to be a profit centre for them but instead would have an impact on people in a meaningful way, and that there were specific tasks and deliverables. In Kazi's case, his executive management at Intel needed to understand that he would spend a percentage of his time on Grameen Intel to run the venture, which was the portion of his time that would not be spent on other for-profit business. There was an opportunity cost to that, which had to be acknowledged and approved. Proactive planning and communication always need to be key focus areas of any intrapreneurs working in a corporate environment with competing priorities.

Avoiding the Endless Pilot

Most of those who work in large corporations have a core set of products that bring in most of the profits. A business can then use some of that money to conduct pilots. Because the focus of the company continues to be on the core products, these pilots become side projects. Pilots can go on forever, and they continue to be pilots. This drains the company's time and resources, and all too often a pilot is considered a success simply because it worked. Grameen Intel was designed from the start to avoid the pitfall of the endless pilot. It was not going to be another corporate social responsibility endeavour, but a real company, with real products, that was run like a real company. There were metrics to measure product adoption and performance, and metrics to measure social impact; an ownership structure for the shareholders to hold management accountable; and a finite amount of money, in this case equity capital, which gave the company a timeline to become self-sustaining.

Grameen Intel was incorporated, shares issued, accounting books established, staff hired, and solutions designed. An office was set up in Bangladesh, where the initial target areas—and Dr Yunus—were located. The company could not have a fancy headquarters in Silicon Valley or Washington DC dispersing programme funds remotely halfway across the world and still claim to be made up of 'do-gooders'. They had to work in the field, in proximity to the problems they sought to address and the customers they hoped to serve.

Product development, in this case software for eAgro and health, could be slow going given the amount of effort needed. Once they had a product, there was a lot of excitement that things would move faster because the customers would want it. However, Kazi and Narayan realized that sales and growth were still slow because what they thought was a need did not necessarily translate to a want (a demand). There was always more to do. They needed to market the solution in remote areas in a way that customers could relate to.

In Grameen Intel's case, the time frame to make a decision on whether their product and business model would succeed, therefore, took longer. That was because of the type of customers and markets they dealt with, where there was little precedence when it came to information technology. Asking them to pay for information was like asking them to pay for air. As Kazi puts it, this 'didn't fit with what a typical MBA programme will teach about market size, market share and a go-to-market strategy'. This was more iterative and exploratory. Entering numbers in a spreadsheet might sound foolish in this environment, but they still did. Not because it gave Kazi and Narayan an answer but because it helped them capture initial assumptions and document changes along the way. Products had to be developed, marketed and adapted to meet real demand.

Tracking Vaccinations

Developing a children's vaccine tracker, called *dolnā*, was a case in point for the extra time and uncertainty involved in developing a product for a social business. Kazi and Narayan had attended a meeting in Delhi with the Gates Foundation in 2010, when the foundation hosted a workshop on their Vaccine Delivery Innovation Initiative. Children worldwide needed vaccinations, but there were few centralized or automated tracking systems to ensure vaccinations were timely. There was also a need to ensure that demand for vaccines could be forecasted beforehand to ensure availability at a local clinic. After the workshop, Kazi and Narayan went back to the US and had their team in Bangladesh design a software application that could be installed on computers at local village health clinics.

The *dolnā* application was built on the *shumātā* platform for maternal healthcare. When a child was born, the nurse would register the child in the database. Based on the date of birth, it would automatically generate a twenty-four-month vaccination schedule for the child. It would then alert the clinic personnel as to which children in the village were due for vaccination on any given day, so that nurses could visit that particular household. Height and weight would also be captured during the vaccination visit, providing additional health records for that child. If the household owned a mobile phone, they could receive an automatic text alert informing them of the need for vaccination. All in all, it was a simple application but with the potential for large impact.

When Grameen Intel developed the *dolnā* vaccine tracker, it was a step forward. When the company tried to deploy the product for the first time at a village clinic, it was adopted but not used—it was a step backward. They had explained the rationale and how it could be used to serve their customers but returned to find that nobody at the clinic had communicated the decision, or even knew which clinic administrator had to sign off. This was a clinic with three nurses in a community of 20,000, a tiny pilot, and yet they could not even get to the point of deciding who would use the software, how data was logged, who would view it, and what kind of analysis should be done in what cadence.

Building a project for a social business, as with any successful business, had to be highly iterative, and the team needed the grit and patience to see it through. More importantly, they needed to understand their customers on a much deeper level. What do they know that is a fact? And what is it that they believe, but isn't true? Do they know their child needs nine vaccinations in a twelve-month window? Do they believe vaccinations are not effective? If these fundamental issues were not addressed as part of educating customers and creating new markets, Grameen Intel didn't have a real business focused on social impact.

That was part of the 'long start-up', a term coined by Patrick Maloney in private conversation to describe the difference in timescale between tech start-ups (the quintessential 'lean start-up') and social enterprise start-ups. A social entrepreneur would still succeed or fail on the strength of their model and demand from their customers, but they could not give up early or pivot away to a more profitable or less challenging problem—but only to a more effective way of addressing that problem. With a time frame that might be twice as long as a tech start-up for determining the viability of a concept, a patient entrepreneur is needed, as well as patient venture capital to invest over that period. Enter the impact investor.

Impact Investing

Antony Bugg-Levine and Jed Emerson defined 'impact investing' in their book of the same name thus: 'Impact investors intend to create positive impact alongside various levels of financial return, both managing and measuring the blended value they create' (2011). This description is deceptively succinct because it encapsulates four major concepts: positive impact, intentionality, management and measurement.

Positive impact is critical. Many investments may, through the organizations they fund, help create positive impact, negative impact or (more likely) both at once. The most common positive impacts of an investment may be increased employment, greater consumer benefits from products or services, and an expanded tax base for the government. However, the intention of venture capitalists is seldom to create positive impact and minimize negative impact; it is typically to generate the best possible financial return for the investors.

The intentionality of the investment is therefore important. If you give money to a company in a way that results in greater positive impacts, but the primary goal of your investment is not to maximize those benefits, you're not an impact investor. Incidental good isn't good enough. However, impact investors still expect 'various levels of financial return', which separates them from donors who expect no financial return. However, an impact investor's expectation of return may be adjusted based not only on the risk of the investment but the expected impact as well, based on their intentions.

Of course, we all know the saying about 'good intentions'. Those intentions are a necessary but not sufficient condition for impact investing. They must also guide the management of the investment to help secure the desired impacts, with the investor as an active participant in the process—no blind trust here. Active management implies adopting responsibility for outcomes created, which was one of J. Gregory Dees' key traits of a social entrepreneur.

Therefore, the impact investor actively seeks to help create positive impact, but how do they know when they've succeeded? Accurate measurement is the final piece of the puzzle. The 'blended value', or triple bottom line, of economic, social and environmental impact created through impact investing is much more challenging to measure than financial returns, but no less important. Although impact measurement is still a nascent field, a number of widely accepted frameworks and approaches have begun to take shape that provide an accounting of social, environmental and economic impact in the same way that traditional methods track financial returns. Some of these methods will be discussed in a later chapter.

All of these factors contribute to the 'additionality' of impact investments when compared to traditional investing. Bugg-Levine and Emerson argue that additionality requires 'investors to target businesses that would not otherwise be capitalized by private investors' (2011). Because the simplest definition of impact in the international development or social enterprise space is what happened only because of your involvement, or the difference between the world as it is and how it would be if you and your organization had never existed (let's call it the 'It's a Wonderful Life' test), additionality ensures real impact. It also differentiates impact investing from other forms of positive investment. Socially responsible investing, for example, is often confused with impact investing because it, too, intentionally seeks positive impact, but the socially responsible investor may not manage the process as closely nor measure the results as clearly.

Additionality

Socially responsible investments historically began as a 'negative screen' in the nineteenth century with investors intentionally divesting from businesses that supported slavery. More than a century later, negative screens took the form of divestment from firms that conducted business in apartheid-era South Africa, sold harmful products such as guns and tobacco, or engaged in practices that accelerated climate change or abused workers. 'Positive screen' investments began to take hold more recently, with investees selected on the basis of their positive impacts, which entailed some measurement. However, socially responsible investing has always lacked additionality because many of the investments are in firms that have many other available avenues for funding, and the causal link from investment to impact is therefore largely impossible to prove.

Because of the importance of additionality in true impact investing, there has been debate in the industry about whether or not impact investments should seek a financial return comparable to that of traditional investments, or whether they must sacrifice some financial return in exchange for greater social or environmental impact. After all, a social enterprise will often reinvest its profits in furthering its mission, and a social business is defined, in part, by the fact that it won't pay a profit to investors. However, a 2015 study of 557 impact investments by fifty-three private equity funds found they produced a rate of financial return nearly identical to that of market indexes for publicly traded stocks (Gray). That's not to say that all impact investments seek a market-rate return, or even should, since many investments with an outsize potential for social and environmental impact often take place in new markets with higher risk. But, it means that market-rate returns are possible for investors with those goals.

The possibility of those returns has lured more and more traditional funds and investors into impact investing, with the result that the number and size of investments have grown dramatically in recent years. The Global Impact Investing Network's annual survey found that more than $15.7 billion was placed in new impact investments in 2015, and that nearly $116 billion in total had been placed in impact investments just by survey respondents (Mudaliar, 2016). It's clear that investors have an interest in blended value, but are there enough market-rate opportunities to meet demand? A trend has already emerged of funds using the term 'impact investment' in ways that clearly fail to meet Emerson and Bugg-Levine's definition, probably as a ploy to improve their brand and attract more investors. Whether the mainstream has the patience, and intention, to invest over longer time frames in highly impactful businesses remains to be seen.

Of course, determining what type of, and how much, positive social and environmental impacts a social enterprise creates is critical to both understanding and analysing the success of that venture as well as its impact investors. It also serves as an important proof point to bring more investors into the field. How can an investor know that they are achieving intended impacts with the same certainty with which they can measure a profit? The emerging field of impact measurement held the key, and it was an approach that Grameen Intel was eager to employ in proving the value of their model to staff, investors and global partners.

Key Lessons:

- Idealism is your North Star, but start with the realities on the ground and the money and capacity you need to get to the desired end state.
- Think like a business start-up, so your concept doesn't become just another pilot project.
- Focus on money, employees, product, customer and impact.

NINE

Many Facts, One Truth

When someone talks about the 'impact' of their job or company, they typically mean the difference they can make on outcomes and results. The impact of an assembly line at GM is the number of cars assembled in a given day. A for-profit company would measure their impact by the profit they made in a given quarter and the financial impact for their shareholders as measured by earnings per share. Anyone associated with an enterprise or business, whether they are employees, customers or shareholders, wants a quantifiable measure of the impact that the organization is having. Without it, why would they be interested in getting involved? Why would anybody fund an organization without these quantifiable goals and measures? But there are more ways to measure the impact of a business than just profitability. Which types of impact are measured, and how they are measured, should depend on the mission of the company.

One of the greatest challenges faced by any social entrepreneur is how to measure the impact of their work around their particular social or environmental cause. What is the truth, the impact of the work, and what are the facts to support it? An organization's financial performance is relatively easy to track, due in part to the thicket of government regulations and industry guidelines around how a corporation or non-profit should report their financials and other governance matters—follow the rules, fill out the right forms and submit to the appropriate regulatory bodies. Other types of impact, although just as important for a social business or non-profit, are harder to measure. How do you know when you've helped someone escape poverty? If they're not hungry, is that because your technology helped them grow more crops, or because the weather was better that year? Does the precise use of fertilizers have an environmental impact due to avoidance of excessive chemicals? If a woman's pregnancy was risk-free, is that due to improved communication between community health workers and a regional doctor, or just good luck? Without such measures, it is difficult to understand the performance of a social enterprise. Setting goals and measuring progress against social and environmental goals for a social enterprise should be taken as seriously as a for-profit company tracking their financials and closely monitoring and managing them to maximize their economic goals.

For example, Grameen Danone, a social business based in Bangladesh, produces yogurt containing essential micronutrients (e.g. calcium, vitamins, iron) that are often lacking in local children. Each cup is sold at an equivalent of less than $0.50. Not only does Grameen Danone have a goal of improving the health of children in poor communities, they also have a goal of reducing poverty through creating employment by sourcing milk locally and hiring local door-to-door sales women to sell cups of yogurt. At various times, Danone has brought in independent third parties to measure the improvements in child health and economic impact to the local communities generated by their business. Likewise, Grameen Intel had at various times assessed the impact on crop yields and increased earnings to farmers due to their technology intervention. These activities helped establish the truth and the facts. The challenge is to incorporate such measures as part of ongoing business operations, in addition to rigorous research assessments conducted from time to time.

To ensure that they are creating the change they seek, social entrepreneurs and investors in their organizations have borrowed from the tools of non-profit management, government policymakers and financial analysts to fashion new ways of measuring social and environmental impact. The old complaints that 'you can't measure social benefit', or that 'measurement is too complex and expensive' are no longer true. There are now widely accepted, easy-to-learn, credible and free methods to measure everything from your organization's carbon emissions to the change in someone's income resulting from their education. One of the biggest hurdles is simply to find the right measurement framework for your organization, which first requires a clear understanding of your theory of change.

Theory of Change and Logic Models

A theory of change describes how you will create the change you seek, a sort of 'if, then' statement of social or environmental impact. Grameen Intel's mission statement is 'solving social problems with information technology at affordable prices'. Kazi believed that if they could create IT solutions for problems such as farm productivity or maternal healthcare access, and make those solutions affordable and desirable, then they could bring some of the spectacular advances in recent technology to bear on addressing hunger, poverty and health. One of the most effective ways to describe your theory of change is through a logic model, also called an impact value chain. Much like how a business model explains how you produce and deliver your products or services to customers, a logic model details how you create and deliver social or environmental benefits.

A logic model is typically broken down into five sections: inputs, activities, outputs, outcomes and impact. Impact and outcomes are sometimes combined, and descriptions of each element may vary slightly, but here are the excellent definitions from *Measuring and Improving Social Impacts* by Marc Epstein and Kristi Yuthas (2014). Their descriptions of each element are paraphrased below:

- **Inputs** are the resources and constraints of an organization or programme. Resources can be tangible, such as staff, money and material, or intangible, such as organizational knowledge or culture. Constraints are the internal and external barriers to success, such as government regulations or lack of cash. For Grameen Intel, these included such items as the staff Intel seconded to the business, the investment from Intel Capital, and the support of Grameen Trust and Muhammad Yunus.

- **Activities** are planned, daily work of the organization to achieve its goals, using the resources it has and operating within the constraints it faces. Grameen Intel engaged in the work of developing, testing and selling software and devices.

- **Outputs** are the direct deliverables of the organization, such as the number of gSlate downloads, COEL devices sold, total women helped by shumātā, or number of farmers utilizing *mrittikā* services.

- **Outcomes** measure the intermediate effects on individuals or populations targeted. For Grameen Intel's eAgro product line, this would include items such as improved crop yields for specific farmers, reduced spending on inputs, higher incomes from greater sales, etc.

- **Impacts** are the long-term changes in society or the environment that are the ultimate goals of the organization. At the end of the day, did Grameen Intel successfully reduce global hunger, poverty and illness through their work?

Inputs and activities are easily tracked through an organization's normal accounting and management processes but measuring other elements of a logic model is more challenging. Epstein and Yuthas lay out a data-gathering plan to guide how an organization collects this information: once its goals are known, a related measurement framework and specific indicators can be chosen. These indicators may be developed by the organization, or drawn from globally accepted frameworks such as the Impact Reporting and Investment Standards (IRIS).

The Macro View

Most social enterprises tend to impact their local communities. When we talk about the rule of one, we are also referring to focusing on one community at a time. However, these goals need to be connected at a broader level that the world recognizes and cares about. Without those global links, the real impact story of a social enterprise will remain isolated and incomplete. Grameen Intel had aligned with the UN MDGs to guide product development and impact measurement, and had originally selected three key goals:

- MDG 1, to eradicate extreme poverty and hunger;
- MDG 2, to achieve universal primary education; and
- MDG 5, to improve maternal health.

Social impact was measured by Grameen Intel using independent, but related, output metrics: the number of farmers who received soil testing through *mrittikā* and related eAgro services, which related to MDG 1; the total number of gSlate downloads, which mapped against MDG 2; and the number of mothers registered to receive services through *shumātā*, which was linked to MDG 5. COEL sales could also be linked to MDG 5, but this approach had to be modified to fit changing UN standards, as described later.

A data-gathering plan should include a baseline, which can be the current state of the organization's activities or the state of a control population. A target is set for each indicator, with progress measured against the baseline. Information on this progress should be collected from specified data sources at a certain frequency. These data also need to be both useful and usable. That seems obvious, simplistic even, but it's amazing how many organizations fail to meet these two standards.

Useful data are based on a theory of change, show real impact, and are meaningful. Unless you're Bill Gates,* your resources are limited. You don't want to spend precious time, money and staff effort collecting information totally unrelated to what you do, no matter how good it sounds. By looking closely at a logic model and deciding on the most important things they need to know, organizations can better focus on their effort. Demonstrating real impact is made easier by this type of focus, especially with the recommended baseline or comparison group, much like Grameen Intel did by comparing control plots of land that didn't use *mrittikā* guidance with those that did. The information

---

* If you are, please send us a dust jacket quote.

collected needs to be meaningful to the people helped, by using terms they understand ('grow more crops while saving money'); to the people who give money, by using comparable measurements ('we align with UN standards'); and to peoples' efforts to improve an organization's own impact, by making certain it's actually usable.

Usable data are time bound, accurate and actionable. That means you can take the information you've gathered and utilize it to directly improve your model, products, or services. The data should reflect a recent point in time, not some arbitrary point in the distant past picked to give you the biggest growth percentages. They should also point towards the immediate future and, ideally, provide some predictive power over the long run. They also can't be misleading or incomplete, which can be exceedingly tricky to ensure, but can be helped by relying on skilled professionals or a reputable third-party provider. Grameen Intel, for example, hired trained ethnographers to gather baseline data and user information. Lastly, and most importantly, the data you collect should relate clearly and directly to what your organization does (products, services) and how you do it (model, organization). You can then act on that information with confidence that you have the complete picture, or at least know what's missing from the puzzle and have the right pieces to complete it.

For Grameen Intel, collecting useful and usable data was facilitated by their technology-based approach. Data sources were fairly straightforward, since they directly monitor downloads of gSlate from the Google Play store, women, signed up for *shumātā*, through its client lists, and farmers using eAgro products by database access. These were collected and reported quarterly to the board, along with financial indicators, such as progress towards break-even, and product milestones, with a goal of releasing three or four new products each year. In this way, the social business could add outputs to their monitoring of regular inputs and activities, and some outcomes could be measured through comparative studies of farmers. Impacts would take longer to ascertain, and required different methods than data collection on outputs and outcomes, because Grameen Intel had to prove that any changes over time were a direct result of their actions, and not due to chance, government interventions, the actions of other businesses or non-profits, or any other external factor.

Modern theories of impact measurement are summed up by what we like to call the 'It's A Wonderful Life' approach. If you've somehow avoided this perennial Christmas favourite, it stars James Stewart as down-at-heel banker George Bailey, who is considering suicide as a result of impending financial disaster and possible imprisonment (in the days when that was seen as shameful, rather than an excuse for a massive severance payment). As he stands on a bridge in the snow, bumbling angel Clarence Odbody comes to show him what the world would be like if he had never existed. The successful social entrepreneur is both Clarence and George: they need to prove what the world would be like if their organization had never existed.

As described by Kevin Starr, executive director of the Mulago Foundation, there are three ways to 'show that it was you' (2012): narrative attribution, matched controls and randomized controlled trials:

- **Narrative attribution** is simply a clear description of the change you created and why you or your organization alone deserves credit. It's basically a story describing your impact. It can be cheap, it's widely used, and it can be very effective. Think of all the beautiful videos you've seen of a non-profit's remarkable impacts. However, this approach is basically anecdotal, and virtually unprovable.
- **Matched controls,** the method utilized by Grameen Intel with their farm plots, are more robust and defensible. These look at two similar groups, one who received the product or service in question and one who didn't, to see if there was a measurable difference in the types of outcomes your organization is seeking to create.
- **A randomized controlled trial** (RCT) is the gold standard. In this case, clients or beneficiaries from the exact same population are randomly assigned to either use your product/service or go without. This is complicated, can be expensive, and carries some obvious ethical concerns when dealing with products designed to improve or save lives.

RCTs are common in the pharmaceutical industry, but MIT's Jameel Poverty Action Lab (J-PAL) deserves much of the credit for demonstrating their usefulness in international development. J-PAL conducted a series of such trials designed to measure the impacts of specific approaches to reducing poverty and improving health and education outcomes in fields where only narrative attribution or basic-matched controls had been used in the past. The outcomes were always illuminating, sometimes surprising, and frequently generated controversy, but such a specific approach could only be used effectively to measure certain types of interventions; it's not a silver bullet.

Grameen Intel's approach worked well: a clear data measurement plan, tied to their business and based on their theory of change that utilized matched controls, good data sources, and a globally accepted impact framework. Using indicators that fed into the MDGs enabled them to draw on global research and reporting, further strengthening the accuracy of their impact measurement and reducing costs. The MDGs, though, were not designed to last forever.

Aligning with the Sustainable Development Goals

In 2015, the MDGs ended, leaving Grameen Intel uncertain of whether their initiatives would continue to align with international measurement programmes, UN publicity campaigns, and global funding priorities. The goals had only been designed to drive international development for fifteen years, after which (it was hoped) they would have been met and new goals could be formulated. Indeed, significant progress had been made towards those goals and their component indicators.

Gains were measured against a baseline set in 1990, although much of the most positive changes had taken place after 2000.

In MDGs related to Grameen Intel's work, the number of people living in extreme poverty (defined as less than $1.25 per day) had dropped from roughly 1.9 billion to fewer than 836 million, achieving the target, while the 'working middle class' (earning more than $4 per day) had tripled to more than half the workforce in developing nations. The proportion of people suffering from hunger in developing nations had been reduced from nearly a quarter of the population to less than thirteen per cent, nearly achieving the target. Over the same period, youth literacy rates increased from eighty-three per cent to ninety-one per cent. Maternal mortality dropped by forty-five per cent worldwide, a decrease driven in part by a jump in births attended by a medical professional from fifty-nine per cent to seventy-one per cent, but this was still far from the targeted reduction. Mortality reduction efforts were further hampered by the fact that nearly half of all countries in the world collected no statistics on maternal cause of death. Child mortality rates had also been reduced, but failed to meet targets. Like maternal mortality, socio-economic status and rural/urban divides were closely linked to those outcomes (*United Nations Millennium Development Goals Report*, 2015). The MDGs had served an important purpose but major work still remained on the path to a shared vision of a world without poverty and suffering.

The year that the MDGs ended, the UN agreed to a successor framework, the Sustainable Development

Goals (SDGs), which would follow a similar fifteen-year timeline. Incorporating seventeen goals and 169 targets, the SDGs were significantly more expansive than the MDGs, with targets such as 'industry, innovation and infrastructure' or 'reduced inequalities' (*United Nations 2030 Agenda*, 2015). Whether these would see the same sort of widespread acceptance and support as the MDGs remained an open question, but they provided a path forward for Grameen Intel as it sought to keep its impact indicators aligned with global frameworks. Four of the new goals were relevant:

- SDG 1 to end poverty;
- SDG 2 to end hunger;
- SDG 3 to ensure healthy lives; and
- SDG 4 to provide quality education.

The increased detail of related targets would enable Grameen Intel to map its internal goals more closely against international targets (see Table 2 on page 146).

The benefits of such an alignment between internal goals and international targets became clear when Kazi and Narayan had the opportunity to attend the UN Broadband Commission. The commission was formed in 2010 in response to former UN Secretary-General Ban Ki-moon's effort to meet the MDG targets using the power of information technology and broadband access in developing countries and underserved communities. The commission was an advocacy group with representatives from the private sector, academia and government, as well as high-profile individuals to help spread the message. In 2013, both Dr Yunus and Intel, represented by John Davies, had a seat on the commission, and both were also members of the Grameen Intel board. That year, the commission were to meet in New York City, and Kazi and Narayan were asked to join the Intel delegation to connect with some individuals who had heard about and were interested in their work.

Earlier that year, John Davies had connected Kazi and Narayan with Ivo Ivanovski, the minister of information technology for the Republic of Macedonia. He was very interested in Grameen Intel's eAgro solution, and they followed up with a call. They had spent several days working on a PowerPoint presentation to explain the solution but only a few minutes into the meeting they realized he was not interested in hearing a pitch. Instead, he had done his homework by reviewing the website before the call, and during the meeting fired off several questions to understand exactly how the soil analysis would be done at the field level. He wanted to meet and invited them to Macedonia. As Kazi put it, 'Mr Ivanovski came across as a dynamic leader who wanted to make a difference in his country and saw the potential of IT.' They agreed to meet at the sidelines of the Broadband Commission meeting.

Kazi and Narayan flew to New York City. What they didn't realize was that the meeting was being held at the same time as UN Week, the start of the UN General Assembly session for the upcoming year. Numerous heads of state had arrived to participate in the launch and make opening speeches. In the streets, they could see an increased presence of police and security services with sirens blaring anytime a VIP motorcade passed. At the Roosevelt hotel, where Kazi and Narayan stayed, they saw security details accompanied by bomb-sniffing dogs. It certainly seemed like their technology work and mapping their activities against the MDGs had landed them somewhere important.

The Broadband Commission meeting took place at the Yale Club of New York City. Attending the meeting with John Davies, Kazi and Narayan saw a line-up of impressive individuals sitting around a large conference room: Paul Kagame, the President of Rwanda; Hamadoun Touré, Secretary-General of the ITU (International Telecommunication Union); Carlos Slim, the Mexican business magnate; Professor Jeffrey Sachs, Director of the Earth Institute at Columbia University; Geena Davis, award-winning actress, and many others. Each was accomplished in their own field but came together towards a common goal of using information technology (and broadband) to meet the MDGs.

Kazi and Narayan listened in to sessions on the broadband policies of countries that had been successful with their implementation plans and the obstacles faced when launching such plans. Because Grameen Intel was focused on local work but with an international message, they had earned a ticket to be part of a forum which was much grander in scale than what they were used to. Later, the meeting with Ivo Ivanovski went well, with a commitment to train critical stakeholders in Macedonia on the impact of technology for soil health, who could then further disseminate that knowledge. This also led to a meeting with the Government of Cambodia and IFAD, where Grameen Intel would work in Cambodia to help with their national goal of doubling rice production.

Although Grameen Intel had to adjust some elements of its impact measurement plan to meet the new SDGs, the updated goals were close enough to the company's core mission that they could remain true to their original purpose and still retain alignment with international targets. It was a new challenge, but also an opportunity to more effectively communicate the impact of their products and services as Grameen Intel entered a period of expansion and growth. There were many facts on the ground, but only one truth: that they needed to make a clear impact on reducing poverty by improving incomes, health and education. To do that, Grameen Intel still had to achieve financial self-sufficiency, which could only be done at a larger scale.

Table 2: Sustainable Development Goals and Targets Aligned with Grameen Intel Impacts

SDG 1: End poverty in all its forms everywhere (aligned with mrittikā and other agricultural products)
1.1 By 2030, eradicate extreme poverty for all people everywhere, currently measured as people living on less than $1.25 a day
1.2 By 2030, reduce at least by half the proportion of men, women and children of all ages living in poverty in all its dimensions according to national definitions

SDG 2: End hunger, achieve food security and improved nutrition and promote sustainable agriculture (aligned with mrittikā and other agricultural products)
2.3 By 2030, double the agricultural productivity and incomes of small-scale food producers, in particular women, indigenous peoples, family farmers, pastoralists and fishers, including, through secure and equal access to land, other productive resources and inputs, knowledge, financial services, markets and opportunities for value addition and non-farm employment
2.4 By 2030, ensure sustainable food production systems and implement resilient agricultural practices that increase productivity and production, that help maintain ecosystems, that strengthen capacity for adaptation to climate change, extreme weather, drought, flooding and other disasters and that progressively improve land and soil quality
SDG 3: Ensure healthy lives and promote well-being for all at all ages (aligned with shumātā application and COEL bangle)
3.1 By 2030, reduce the global maternal mortality ratio to less than 70 per 100,000 live births
3.2 By 2030, end preventable deaths of newborns and children under 5 years of age, with all countries aiming to reduce neonatal mortality to at least as low as 12 per 1,000 live births and under-5 mortality to at least as low as 25 per 1,000 live births
SDG 4: Ensure inclusive and equitable quality education and promote lifelong learning opportunities for all (aligned with gSlate)
4.6 By 2030, ensure that all youth and a substantial proportion of adults, both men and women, achieve literacy and numeracy

Source: United Nations. 2015. 'Transforming our world: the 2030 Agenda for Sustainable Development'

Key Lessons:

- Set clear goals for impact, and ensure they're linked to your business model.
- Create a theory of change, logic model and data measurement plan to guide your approach.
- Utilize common or widely accepted frameworks for impact measurement.

TEN

One Byte at a Time

Organizations pursuing social impact make a distinction between scaling their impact and growing the organization. These two things may or may not be related: it's possible to expand the benefit of an organization without actually growing in size, and vice versa. The field of international development is full of stories about organizations that grew in size (and funding) but not in positive impact delivered. One example was the Red Cross Haiti Programme, launched after an earthquake in 2010 that killed up to 300,000 people and displaced a further 1.5 million.* The programme raised $488 million to rebuild permanent homes for the local population through a network of organizations in Haiti. The end result was fewer than a

---

* https://www.cnn.com/2015/06/04/americas/american-red-cross-haiti-controversy-propublica-npr/index.html

dozen permanent homes and many temporary projects that failed to have a lasting impact on the population (Martinez, 2015).

An example more closely related to technology was One Laptop Per Child (OLPC), a non-profit organization that sought to transform global education by developing and distributing computers for school children in developing nations. The first challenge was to develop an inexpensive, rugged, low-power laptop, which involved negotiations with hundreds of parts suppliers. Once the prototype was developed, it then had to be manufactured at scale and distributed through national governments. As of 2007, the non-profit had \$22 million* in cash on hand, mainly received from donor contributions. Many high-tech companies also stepped in to provide support. However, in part due to the challenges of working through a complex network of suppliers and other related to design, OLPC never reached their target of a \$100 price for the laptop. They also faced distribution complications from working with national governments that faced numerous competing agendas. Eventually, the programme did provide millions of computers to children who would not otherwise have had access to one, but the model required extensive subsidization from governments and semi-private organizations to make it work.

Closer to home, on one of John Davies' trips to Bangladesh on behalf of Intel's World Ahead programme, he worked with the government on the need for computers in government-run schools. While the decision and the

---

* Source: OLPC Foundation, 2007 audit report.

fund allocation process by the government dragged on, John agreed to provide 1,000 computers free of cost to demonstrate the possibilities. Unfortunately, the computers could not initially be distributed because the local authorities could not provide a list of the schools where the computers should go. The computers sat in a local distribution centre while the distributor made urgent calls to Intel's local country manager as he tried to free up space for other shipments coming into the warehouse.

Size and impact are often conflated but they are very different. Making a huge donation or pledge isn't the same as creating a small model for sustainable impact that can be replicated thousands of times—the Rule of One. For a social business, however, economies of scale are often necessary to achieve profitability and the financial sustainability it brings. What's important is to ensure that the organization is scaling in the right way at the right time for the right reasons.

The PATRI Framework

Rizwan Tayabali describes an approach for successfully scaling social ventures, either non-profit or for-profit, through the PATRI framework (2014). PATRI stands for 'Purpose, Applicability, Transferability, Readiness and Implementation', a step-by-step process for assessing the ability to scale the impact of an already proven product or service and associated business model. Even for social intrapreneurs like Kazi, embedded within a multinational corporation such as Intel, scaling will take a different form and occur on a different time frame than for the parent organization. Grameen Intel followed the same basic principles as the PATRI framework as they moved to grow their proven solutions.

Purpose: A social venture must be pursuing scale with a clarity of purpose. Are they scaling to help solve the problem they were designed to address, to satisfy external pressure or to appeal to a founder's vanity? For social businesses, with a product or service being sold that is (hopefully) tied directly to proven impact, organizational growth and scaling impact are often linked, but impact should increase at a faster pace than the size of the organization. If it costs the same to deliver the solution to the thousandth customer as to the first, it's clear that the needed efficiencies aren't being achieved. Grameen Intel sought scale because it would help them achieve greater impact through their model as well as the financial sustainability to ensure that the model endured.

Applicability: This reflects the second part of the framework and covers both the impact solution and business model at scale. A solution tailored to a specific region, or one that requires substantial hands-on support for each delivery, may not be suitable for scaling in its current form. Likewise, a business model that isn't designed to grow in efficiency as scale is achieved will only cause problems down the road. Kazi's team had worked from the start to make certain that their software applications were applicable across various regions and cultures, apart from minor translation needs. The business model was designed for scale, with organizational processes, accounting controls, communication and management practices based on those of larger organizations.

Transferability: This careful design enabled Grameen Intel to meet the third part of the framework—transferability and systematization. By creating standardized processes for everything from ethnographic research to product development to delivery and impact measurement, the social business was prepped to replicate its approach in other areas. This reflected Kazi and Narayan's own experience as social intrapreneurs, the skills of their advisers (including Muhammad Yunus), and their careful team selection—all of which also impacted their organizational readiness for scale, the fourth part of the framework.

Readiness: This stage reflects not only the organizational processes and planning necessary for scale but the individual capacity of leaders to learn, grow and adapt. An organization with one employee looks very different from one with one hundred; can an entrepreneur learn to delegate effectively and manage a larger team? In this way, practised intrapreneurs who may be used to managing larger teams and working within existing systems can sometimes be more effective than entrepreneurs who lack such experience.

Implementation: Finally, an organization must have an effective road map for scaling. Once the road map, often conceptualized as a business plan is completed, an organization is ready to seek the necessary human and financial resources, set up operations in readiness for scaling, execute on the plan and monitor results. Grameen Intel had launched with the plan and resources to scale as a result of Kazi's approach and investments from Grameen Trust and Intel Capital. They had set up operations with scaling in mind and now only had to execute. However, that proved harder than expected.

Kazi's objective from day one had been to make Grameen Intel financially sustainable. The idea was not to rely on donor money or grants but that the business should pay for its own expenses. In other words, they had to generate revenue through the sale of their products and services, but at affordable prices. For their eAgro products, the soil health software was sold for $10 to an entrepreneur, or as Kazi put it, the 'soil doctor'. This person also had to purchase a soil-testing kit comprising a briefcase of chemicals and test tubes. The soil doctor could then sell their services to a farmer for $2 to $3 per soil test. For COEL, the carbon monoxide monitoring bangle, Grameen Intel targeted a $14 price point (This is still work in progress).

Grameen Intel's growth target was simply to recoup 100 per cent of their costs assessed through an annual budgeting process with quarterly updates. This yearly budget included more than 100 line items including payroll, office rental, utilities, training, travel and phone bills. Variance from the budgeted amount was tracked closely, reflecting the same accounting controls in place at a traditional for-profit business. Policies and approval processes provided checks and balances* on spending. In a given year early in Grameen Intel's history, cost recovery ranged from five per cent to twenty per cent of total spending.

Reaching 100 per cent would require them to sell more software and more wearables—a simple approach, but one full of execution challenges. On the revenue generation front, ten to twenty key activities were closely tracked. These included items such as field implementation in Cambodia and the status of deploying 290 associated software licences; the number of farmers receiving soil health services; and the progress of meetings with governments in Nigeria or India interested in using their technology solutions. The size of each opportunity, the target date and the next step for how to approach them to move to the next level of discussion were tracked and captured. This followed the same sales pipeline method of any large business.

The possibility of achieving financial break-even was real, helped by a cost structure effected by locating most business operations in low-cost geographies. The targets they needed to hit weren't in the millions of sales but less than 100,000 units of software and wearable devices combined. Grameen Intel's investors had provided nearly eight years of working capital to meet those goals. However, by the end of 2016, they were already at year five.

Faced with the need to jump from twenty per cent cost coverage to 100 per cent in three years, the focus of the business shifted. The bulk of weekly staff meetings

---

* Puns intended.

changed from discussing product concepts to reviewing customer leads. Cost discussions changed from the highest priority for new spending, based on desired business outcomes, to where they could optimize costs further. The dedication to controlling costs extended to office amenities: employees gave up a choice of either coffee or tea and instead opted for just tea, since it was cheaper to only supply one. Kazi and Narayan no longer travelled to international conferences unless they were invited and all of their costs were covered by the organizer (which also signalled that the host valued their presence and contribution).

A fixed amount of working capital was a powerful incentive for management to keep cost recovery at the forefront. Kazi found the behaviour driven by that obligation to be very different from what he saw in a foundation or NGO; instead, it was about survival. His managers realized that the ability to do good meant being smart about finance. By keeping a tight control on costs and being laser focused on generating product sales at affordable prices, they could achieve more with less and create greater positive impact. Financial discipline, cost recovery and differentiated products with clear social benefits and market demand were some of their key tenets. They fell between a traditional for-profit business and a philanthropy but fit right in with other social businesses. Now they just had to realize their potential for growth.

Challenges to Growth

Grameen Intel had started as a test bed for ideas: shumātā, *dolnā*, gSlate, the COEL bracelet and their suite of eAgro apps. This came with a set of operational challenges, since designing new products is a very different process than selling and delivering them. As Kazi put it,

> Most organizations like us get into a cycle of piloting various ideas, and very soon we realized you don't quite get out of that phase. As long as there is funding, this becomes the default operational mode. You feel success is always just around the corner, and you try to engage various other development agencies and NGOs to buy into your ideas under the banner of 'capacity building'.

They were facing the trap of the endless pilot. It didn't take long for them to realize that the sales numbers they needed for survival, which their investors were counting on, simply weren't there. Experimentation was important for their model, but along the way, they learnt three important lessons for growth as they prepped the applicability of their solution and model: addressing pain points, finding focus and ensuring affordability.

Grameen Intel's eAgro apps focused on soil health as an area for addressing a pain point. They had initially conceptualized the software as providing a platform to find competitive prices for seeds and fertilizers and weather forecasts for farmers. But there were similar ideas out there already, including a solution provided by Reuters with mixed commercial success. Soil health was a key pain point: excessive use of fertilizers and suboptimal yields had a direct impact on a farmer's costs and income.

With a key pain point and a solution in mind, they needed focus. Grameen Intel had to get their mindshare and resources behind it. It might sound obvious, but they found it difficult to implement this focus in the business, especially after going through a phase of experimentation. Every discussion would digress into another possible concept, and the danger was that it might become their default operational mode. When discussing the soil health solution deployment, a typical digression would be: 'How about we look at microcredit for purchase of seeds and fertilizer? How about we design a portal that allows a farmer to easily find a source of funding?' Kazi described his typical response as, 'Can we make sure the solution in front of us is first successful?' They realized that good ideas aren't difficult to come up with. There are plenty of good ideas out there but most of them don't get off the ground due to resources being spread too thin across too many trials and experiments. Moving from the 'divergent' phase of Human-Centred Design to the 'convergent' phase was a key challenge.

Then the solution had to be made affordable. When providing soil health services, the intermediary entrepreneur was the most important role. Not every farmer can afford a computing device or a soil-testing kit. However, because the upfront investment in technology could be used multiple times, the fixed cost became affordable. The 'soil doctor' charged $2–$3 for a soil-testing service, which made the technology package affordable. There was also the human factor— helping the farmer to understand and implement the recommendation so that they actually saved money. For example, helping them deal with seed and fertilizer suppliers who were often there to sell bags of supplies and not necessarily to provide knowledge based on the actual needs of the farmer.

Breaking down the 'applicability' phase of planning to scale into addressing pain points, focus and affordability gave Kazi and Narayan key strategies for achieving scale. Grameen Intel was at a phase of their business where they had to remain focused on soil health and their new wearable device—the two most promising avenues for future growth. They were determined to scale based on early success stories and decided not to pursue expansion into new products at that time.

The challenge then became to make those products such a commercial success that they would allow Grameen Intel to recoup operating costs. The final bottleneck, it seemed, was marketing. They could always operate in a handful of villages—their solutions were already deployed across forty-nine locations in Bangladesh. But how could they reach thousands of villages? How could they market their solutions effectively? Placing billboards and radio and TV ads were typical ways to reach rural farmers in Bangladesh, but even with such advertising, they needed to build out the company's capacity to provide services across the entire country.

One inspiration came from Amazon in the US. When you returned a product to Amazon, they gave you a choice of mailing it via UPS or dropping it off at a designated 'lock box'. These were agreements with existing brick-and-mortar companies like Plaid Pantry. The Amazon website listed options for these various drop-off locations close to the user. Kazi and Narayan realized that this type of partnership was replicable in developing nations; for example, telecom companies had existing locations across Bangladesh. These had independent agents who offered cell phone repairs or could load prepaid minutes on to a phone in exchange for cash. Grameen Intel reached out to the second-largest telecom operator in Bangladesh, Robi Axiata, which had 3,000 such centres.

They envisioned two types of services with Robi. A farmer could call a help desk and receive a generic recommendation on the amount of fertilizer that was specific to the crop and general soil conditions for their geo-climatic zone. This information came from a database that Grameen Intel had compiled based on publicly available data. The cost to the farmer was a few cents that they had to spend for air time and call centre service. If the farmer was interested in a more specific analysis, they would have the option to have a soil-health analysis done for their specific plot through a local service centre.

Kazi met with Robi in December 2016, along with the team who would implement the solution, and found a relatable approach to business. Their CEO quickly jumped into the practical side of things: What problem were they solving? How? How does a farmer get access? At what price? Is it affordable? Would the farmer see an impact in return for their spending? How would they train people to offer these solutions? These were all questions that Kazi could answer because of Grameen Intel's earlier emphasis on addressing real pain points, focusing the business model and ensuring affordability.

The purpose of Grameen Intel in pursuing scale was twofold: success meant achieving impact numbers and securing the company's financial health—linked goals that both required growth. A few farmers gaining access to computerized soil analysis or a handful of mothers wearing a device that addressed their health concerns was a good thing. Impacting 10,000 people who used their solution was a great thing, but impacting 100,000 people was even better. Success meant hitting the right impact numbers, which would also make the company financially sustainable. That sustainability would enable the company to continue to create social good over a long term.

Kazi identified Grameen Intel's key challenges in achieving the pace of scale they desired as an overemphasis on design and the cultural fit for new employees: 'We were not quick enough to stop the flow of ideas and get our focus on two to three key products, which we could have done two years earlier.' This hampered their focus and ability to bear down on the applicability of the impact solution. They also focused early hiring too much on candidates who shared their values for creating social good. While this seemed like an important consideration, they realized, 'instead we needed a few individuals with a track record of building successful marketing and sales channels'. New partnerships helped to overcome this gap, from working with the Robi Axiata CEO to Cambodia's secretary of state in the ministry of agriculture, who was focused on making the country a major exporter of rice. He was able to help Grameen Intel link a macro-level challenge to micro-level implementation, training local agricultural extension offices in the use of their technology solutions.

Scaling Grameen Intel was still a work in progress, with a renewed need to focus on marketing and sales efforts while engaging with influencers. The impact was proven, and the business model had been designed and refined to support that impact, but without scale driven by growth, the company couldn't become financially sustainable. There were no grants or donors to fall back on; the social business had to live or die on its own.

Key Lessons:

- To prepare for scaling, first you need to address customer pain points, focus on the appropriate product and business model, and ensure affordability for customers.
- Scaling is different from growth, because you can scale impact without growing your organization, so be clear on your goals.

ELEVEN

Everyone's an Entrepreneur

When Craig Barrett initially proposed setting up Grameen Intel with Muhammad Yunus, there were a few value drivers that were relevant for Intel. One was the partnership with a Nobel Laureate to make their technology more impactful. The Bangladesh market alone was not large enough for Intel to be interested, but solving real problems that billions of people faced in some of the most impoverished parts of the world was important. As long as the technology had relevance to one more poor person, that was good enough. And who else was a better spokesperson for the poor than Yunus, the father of microcredit?

At an individual level, Kazi and Narayan saw a similar opportunity. Their business and technical skills would go towards something they believed was useful, in addition to their day jobs of 'maximizing shareholder return'. They would gain the valuable experience of starting a company to address some of the most pressing problems in the world. It would involve hiring, management, research and design, and sales—a holistic skill set any aspiring manager would seek to develop. On top of that, as a finance professional, Kazi would learn more about working in emerging markets, legal entity structures, shareholding rules and dealing with regulatory bodies.

From a mentoring standpoint, they had two public figures to guide them: Craig Barrett and Muhammad Yunus. Craig Barrett impressed on them the importance of taking a broad view of solving problems: how poverty was linked to issues such as a country's education policy or broadband access. Yunus, on the other hand, coached them on ground-level realities, such as why simple and targeted communications were critical for their customer segment or how business savvy the poor really are. You cannot simply try to sell them a low-cost solution (for example, a soil test) and promise an outcome a few months later (higher crop yields). Kazi and Narayan needed to get smart on the value proposition and communicate that in a way that resonated enough for customers to pay for it.

The impact to their careers would involve building up core skills relevant to their profession while gaining access to two famous individuals, the movers and shakers in their industry. As Kazi put it, 'Very few of my finance peers got such an opportunity to do something as broad.' As a social intrapreneur, he had access to capital, markets, staff and mentors that even the most successful social entrepreneurs often lack—not to mention a regular pay cheque. But there were downsides to working within an existing organization. As Kazi described it:

> It was great to be left alone to drive new ideas and innovation. However, in a large corporation, the entrenched players continue on their existing path, gaining more experience on a portfolio of big projects tied to the core business. So, in a way, we moved away from the traditional career ladder. In order to maintain the linkage back to the core, we've had to go find ways to remain visible and to rationalize the ongoing work.

Start-up ventures often make an effort to be immediately visible even before having a product or a success story. Kazi believed, it was instead important to focus on quiet execution without a lot of fanfare especially early on in the process. But patience varies widely among higher management, so they faced the perennial risk of all intrapreneurs that funding would be cancelled prematurely. It became a balance between making scarce time available for internal public relations efforts and ensuring a certain level of progress. They had to find some avenues for visibility, at least in the early stages, to keep the work alive.

At Intel's 2014 Development Forum, Kazi was invited as a keynote speaker to talk about Grameen Intel's technology solutions. This was an annual event attended by thousands of developers who gathered to share ideas on new technologies. Kazi did an onstage demo of the eAgro software and highlighted some of the outcomes in

Cambodia as a result of using technology for more precise application of fertilizers: 7.6 per cent less investment in fertilizers coupled with a twenty-six per cent increase in yields. Dr Hermann Eul, an Intel vice president, summarized their work as creating an all-new ecosystem with tremendous opportunity for entrepreneurs and innovators to solve some of the world's biggest problems. In 2016, an article on the COEL bangle was published on the company's intranet, visible to 100,000 Intel employees worldwide. It narrated the story in a way a Western audience would understand, and helped build the internal case for Grameen Intel's work.

From a career development standpoint, during the start-up phase of the business, which lasted close to three years, they tried to maintain internal visibility by taking on special projects. Kazi took on a three-month project on customer segmentation related to Intel's server business. For Narayan, it was sales and marketing. He was linked into the World Ahead programme to help drive broadband access, which in turn would enable higher computer usage. This was not very different from the start-up social entrepreneur holding down a day job to make ends meet, as Kazi explained:

In other words, being visible to those in the core business who were making decisions on your next promotion by itself became a part-time job. In our case, neither Barrett nor Yunus had any regular interaction with our functional leaders back at Intel. If they did, they were talking about issues tied to the core business. Remember that Grameen Intel is a stand-alone company with a separate board. That's where the buck stops, and so do discussions about performance reviews and career progression.

Over time, this became more and more challenging for Kazi and Narayan. They maintained ongoing involvement with Grameen Intel but focused more on developing the in-country management team who 'could be the de facto Kazi and Narayan'. To succeed as an intrapreneur within a large organization, building up a local team over time is often the only option to ensure success—the 'scale' stage of embedding an intrapreneurial endeavour, in Croll and Yoskovitz's framework. However, the higher-level issue that Kazi felt was being overlooked was the impact of their contributions back to Intel:

Corporations have to realize the broad skills that one acquires doing these projects can be very valuable to the core business. For example, we'd like to see CSR [Corporate Social Responsibility] activities get revamped based on our experience, not just at Intel but in the industry as a whole. Grameen Intel spends a fraction of the overall CSR budget of any large corporation, but our approach can redefine how we think about CSR. Social responsibility should be defined by extending our core technology products for social good.

Another area where these skills could be highly relevant to a core business is in emerging business units or projects in various stages of incubation. How do you get a new programme set up within a large corporation to launch a different set of products and services? How do you define investment amounts at various phases of the business? How do you think about new sets of customers? Kazi and Narayan were able to find answers for Intel on how to effectively conduct business in emerging markets where the majority of the world population lives. It was critical that these acquired skills were highlighted and linked back to the core business. Maybe the old way of doing things could not always be the prescription for future success.

Kazi and Narayan's experience in moving Grameen Intel from start-up to an operational phase added to the breadth and depth of business knowledge at Intel. They needed to be entrepreneurs within a large corporation, which by itself is a key skill in modern organizations. In Kazi and Narayan's case, they needed to work with the top decision makers, and it required them to understand organizational priorities and identify ways for their work to serve the core mission. It is one thing to talk about innovation and globalization but another to have done it in practice. Their experience showed them how some of the core technologies on which a Fortune 500 company spends billions of dollars to develop could be extended for social impact.

Kazi and Narayan's work gave them a unique perspective on the real needs of people in some of the most impoverished parts of the world. Through the course of working through these solutions, they would be the first to admit that they underestimated the challenges involved and idealized the solutions they generated. Most multinational companies are guilty of those same habits. As a group, they tend to get carried away with market growth and the euphoria of the impact on the next billion people. Instead, why not expand existing CSR programmes to incorporate the development and launch of social business concepts? These could start small as a stand-alone unit or subsidiary with a focus on extending a company's core competency for social impact and with a goal towards long-term financial sustainability. Once the model was proven on a small scale, it could be scaled using the company's existing infrastructure.

The Future of Grameen Intel

Although it was important not to continuously launch new products without establishing the success of past items, Kazi and Narayan had to balance a disciplined approach with the need to act on new opportunities. Continued focus on the existing set of products— digital soil-testing kit, eAgro suite, and COEL, and scaling their impact still forms the core of the effort. But, they are also constantly looking to what additional opportunities exist to drive sustainable social impact. As part of their local agricultural services, one of Grameen Intel's corporate customers introduced water pumps to irrigate agricultural lands. They covered sixteen districts and served a population of approximately 190,000. In some of the sites, the pumps broke after a day of continuous operation, but the motor continued to run, wasting precious fuel. The Grameen Intel team devised a solution with an electronic sensor that automatically shuts off the pump if it overheats, avoiding breakage. If it senses no flow of water, the fuel cuts off the motor automatically. This avoided costly replacements of the pump and reduced fuel waste. Another customer leased tractors for farming through a monthly payment system. To minimize theft and credit risk, they asked Grameen Intel for a way to track the tractor, monitor engine usage, and have the ability to remotely shut it down if needed. A creative use of sensor data connectivity made all this possible.

Under the leadership of Zia Manzur, who has a sales background and is the head of operations, both of these solutions became revenue-generating projects for the company, helping it move closer to financial sustainability. Grameen Intel continues to take a market sensing and product development role. They planted a seed and demonstrated the possibilities of creative uses of technology. Now, the Grameen Intel team sees a tremendous opportunity for thousands of these solutions, not only in Bangladesh and India, but also throughout Africa and Latin America. We are also using a new brand, Technology for Social Impact (TSI), which reflects the true nature of our cause instead of the names of the founding shareholders.

In conclusion

To have a real impact on economic development, companies need to focus on creating the next set of products and services that will help drive the world's growth. This should involve lifting billions of people out of poverty. Kazi and Narayan learnt a few key points about solving big problems when they set up Grameen Intel. First, most companies aim too high. It's not about trying to solve world hunger. As former Intel CEO Craig Barrett often used to say, based on a bit of wisdom he found in a fortune cookie: 'A small deed done is better than a big deed planned.' Second, financial numbers are good, but building up practical knowledge and pragmatic solutions in these markets will have greater positive impact over time. Both of these aspects are often overlooked.

Today, both Kazi and Narayan are part of the senior leadership at Intel but remain committed to the mission they started. Grameen Intel was an off-the-beaten-track project that was difficult to pass up. They could use our technology and business skills to get in on the ground floor of a venture capital investment, take a company from concept to viable entity, and build local capacity for social impact in a developing country.

Beyond personal growth, learning opportunities and new career pathways, the impetus to address major problems is the overriding drive for social intrapreneurs. As Kazi put it, 'Let's not forget that getting a company off the ground and developing real products is a lot of hard work.' Staying motivated to create a new path within an organization takes reflection and purpose. 'As intrapreneurs, we wanted to add value in the way we think about people and economics. This, we felt, was the only way to reach the next five billion people on this earth with information technology as a force for change for the better.'

Addressing this emerging marketplace will take entrepreneurs and intrapreneurs to challenging parts of the world. They need to remember that innovation in this sector isn't driven by corporate brainstorming sessions, PowerPoint strategies, abstract theories or fancy concepts. It takes real, tactical work. When starting a social business, entrepreneurs need to have a real understanding of the people in developing countries and the struggles they face before they can decide how best to deliver a real service to them.

TWELVE

Educator's Guide

Social entrepreneurship has taken the world by storm, from bestselling books by Muhammad Yunus to an explosion of academic programmes: half the top fifty business schools in the world now 'host a social impact programme, initiative, or centre', according to the Skoll Foundation (Ditkoff, 2017). Ashoka U, the university arm of the global Ashoka organization that recognizes and supports leading social entrepreneurs, found that the number of social entrepreneurship offerings at colleges and universities grew 200 per cent in the five years to 2013 (2014). All institutions in the Ashoka U Changemaker Campus Consortium, recognized as the top universities in the world teaching social entrepreneurship, have one or more courses on a related topic. Outside this network, Harvard, Duke, Oxford and University of Cape Town have required courses or related content in their graduate business schools (Ditkoff, 2017).

This increase is driven by both student and employer demand. Net Impact, a global organization for business students interested in social and environmental sustainability, reported that seventy-two per cent of university students said that making a positive difference through their job was an important life goal, a higher percentage than those who listed having children or a prestigious career (Zukin, 2012). Meanwhile, more and more employers are requesting that new hires demonstrate competency in '21st-Century Skills' that align almost exactly with change-maker skills taught in university social entrepreneurship courses. Unfortunately, many social entrepreneurship books, articles and curricula assume that the reader or student will go on to start their own venture, rather than pursuing meaningful impact in a job at an existing organization. Not all those interested in social entrepreneurship want to, can, or should start a new organization. Enter social intrapreneurship, and the purpose of this book.

The Rule of One was designed in part as a learning tool for college and university students studying social intrapreneurship, aspiring or practising social intrapreneurs and programme managers at government agencies or non-profits. As a relatively new field, social intrapreneurship lacks many of the resources available in related areas, and this text is meant to fill part of that gap. Co-author Jacen Greene teaches social intrapreneurship at Portland State University, an Ashoka U Changemaker Campus, and has incorporated some of the theories and resources taught in his courses throughout the text. These resources draw on extensive interviews, research and curriculum review in this emerging field. Likewise, co-authors Kazi I. Huque and Narayan Sundararajan bring their own experience as practising social intrapreneurs, and their close association with experts like Muhammad Yunus, to inform the applied elements of the text.

This educator's guide provides a detailed reference for how this book can be used in educational settings or reading groups. This includes associated readings, videos and resources that serve as valuable supplementary material, as well as reading guides and discussion questions for each chapter. The authors hope that educators, practitioners, students and others will use this guide to help them inspire, and become, the next wave of successful social intrapreneurs.

General Material

Building Social Business: The New Kind of Capitalism that Serves Humanity's Most Pressing Needs by Muhammad Yunus and Karl Weber is a useful guide to Yunus's philosophy and approach. It includes Yunus's original definition of 'social business', a guide on starting a social business and descriptions of the Grameen-affiliated social businesses started at that point. An essential text on the subject.

'Grameen Intel Social Business: Technology Solutions at the Base of the Pyramid' is an award-winning academic case study on Grameen Intel by Jacen Greene, Dr Theodore Khoury and Cindy Cooper. The case uses the Grameen Intel story as a starting point for advanced undergraduate or graduate students to develop a plan to launch an intrapreneurial endeavour, create a market entry strategy for a business serving the base of the pyramid, and design an impact measurement plan. The case teaching note includes links to a set of associated videos. The case is available at https://wdi-publishing.com/product/grameen-intel-social-business-technology-solutions-at-the-base-of-the-pyramid.

The League of Intrapreneurs, a membership-based organization, is created in partnership with a number of international impact, banking and development organizations. The League offers events, connections and resources for social intrapreneurs, including the excellent (and somewhat frighteningly titled) 'Cubicle Warriors Toolkit'.

- https://www.leagueofintrapreneurs.com/2017/02/06/league-intrapreneurs-toolkit-sharing-lessons-field/

Chapter 1: Time Is More than Money

Questions for Discussion:
1. What are some possible shortcomings of the social enterprise movement?
2. Are there areas in which a social enterprise approach may be especially needed? Areas in which it would not be appropriate?

Recommended Reading:
- Fisher, Martin. 'Income Is Development'. *MIT Innovations*. Winter 2006. https://www.mitpressjournals.org/doi/abs/10.1162/itgg.2006.1.1.9

Chapter 2: Think Like an Entrepreneur Inside Your Organization

Questions for Discussion:
1. Are corporations still as inflexible in their acceptance of intrapreneurs as Pinchot believed they were in the late 1970s?
2. Who is a good example of a social intrapreneur in your field?

Recommended Reading:
- Dees, J. Gregory. 'The Meaning of Social Entrepreneurship'. Stanford University. https://entrepreneurship.duke.edu/news-item/the-meaning-of-social-entrepreneurship/

Chapter 3: Spend Time in the Field and Learn from Small Successes

Questions for Discussion:
1. Have you ever been treated with empathy from someone working for a large organization, such as a business, non-

profit, university or the government? How did it affect your interactions with that organization?

2. How might you adopt a 'beginner's mindset' in your own work or pursuits?

Recommended Reading:
- 'Design Kit'. IDEO.org. http://www.designkit.org
- 'Sustainable Development Goals'. United Nations. https://sustainabledevelopment.un.org

Chapter 4: Keep Solutions Real

Questions for Discussion:
1. Does business, even social business or social enterprises, have a role to play in reducing poverty? If so, how is that role distinct from that of aid organizations, government or churches and charities?
2. Would it benefit non-business organizations to create a business model describing how they create, deliver and capture value? Are there specific sectors or organizations for which this might be especially useful?

Recommended Reading:
- Banerjee, Abhijit V., and Esther Duflo. 2011. *Poor Economics: A Radical Rethinking*

> of the Way to Fight Global Poverty. New
> York: PublicAffairs.
> - Polak, Paul, and Mal Warwick. 2013. *The
>   Business Solution to Poverty: Designing
>   Products and Services for Three Billion
>   New Customers*. San Francisco: BK.
> - Osterwalder, Alexander, and Yves Pigneur.
>   2010. *Business Model Generation: A
>   Handbook for Visionaries, Game Changers,
>   and Challengers*. Hoboken: Wiley.
>
> **Chapter 5: Less Is More, Focus Is Key**
>
> Questions for Discussion:
> 1. Given the savvy cost-benefit calculations
>   of people living in the villages surveyed
>   by Grameen Intel, what are some other
>   opportunities for social businesses to
>   develop a product/service to sell there that
>   would increase local incomes?
> 2. What are some potential complications or
>   challenges with Grameen Intel's *shumātā*
>   healthcare programme?
>
> Recommended Reading:
> - Boo, Katherine. 2012. *Behind the Beautiful
>   Forevers: Life, Death, and Hope in a
>   Mumbai Undercity*. New York: Random
>   House.

Chapter 6: Simplicity Is Complex

Questions for Discussion:
1. What are some areas of skeuomorphic design in your own life? Are they used appropriately?
2. How would the concept of virality translate from business intrapreneurship to realms like government or education?

Recommended Reading:
- 'Household (Indoor) Air Pollution'. World Health Organization. https://www.who.int/phe/air/en/

Chapter 7: Create Income, Not Consumption

Questions for Discussion:
1. Is it morally defensible for a social business to pursue a course of action that may benefit a larger number of people even while disadvantaging a few of its older customers, as in the case of Grameenphone? If so, when? What are the limits?
2. Are there other areas of international development or social entrepreneurship where organizations should be actively pursuing their own obsolescence or transformation?

Recommended Reading:
- Shaffer, Richard. 'Unplanned Obsolescence'. *Fast Company*, September 2007. https://www.fastcompany.com/60302/unplanned-obsolescence

Chapter 8: Patient Capital, Patient Entrepreneurs

Questions for Discussion:
1. Is it appropriate for investors to seek outcomes beyond financial returns?
2. Do you have any sustainable investments or impact investments? If so, what criteria did you use when making those investments?

Recommended Reading:
- Bugg-Levine, Antony, and Jed Emerson. 2011. 'Impact Investing: Transforming How We Make Money While Making a Difference'. Hoboken: Jossey-Bass.

Chapter 9: Many Facts, One Truth

Questions for Discussion:
1. What's the theory of change and logic model for your organization?
2. Does your organization measure and report non-financial impacts? If so, how?

3. Are the Sustainable Development Goals an effective replacement for the Millennium Development Goals?

Recommended Reading:

- Epstein, Marc J., and Kristi Yuthas. 2014. *Measuring and Improving Social Impacts: A Guide for Nonprofits, Companies, and Impact Investors*. San Francisco: Berrett-Koehler.
- 'The Millennium Development Goals Report 2015'. United Nations. 2015. http://www.un.org/millenniumgoals/2015_MDG_Report/pdf/MDG%202015%20rev%20(July%201).pdf
- 'Transforming Our World: The 2030 Agenda for Sustainable Development'. United Nations. http://www.un.org/ga/search/view_doc.asp?symbol=A/RES/70/1&Lang=E

Chapter 10: One Byte at a Time

Questions for Discussion:
1. What's an example of an organization that grew in size without scaling positive impact commensurately? What about an organization that scaled positive impact dramatically faster than it grew?
2. In your opinion, was Grameen Intel pursuing the best avenues for scaling? Why or why not?

Recommended Reading:
- Tayabali, Rizwan. 2014. 'PATRI Framework for Scaling Social Impact'. Ashoka Globalizer. https://issuu.com/ashokachangemakers/docs/patri-framework

Chapter 11: Everyone's an Entrepreneur

Questions for Discussion:
1. Are there areas in which encouraging entrepreneurial thinking isn't desirable?
2. How might you act more entrepreneurially in your pursuits, or enable others to do so?

Recommended Reading:
- 'Cubicle Warriors Toolkit'. League of Intrapreneurs. https://www.leagueofintrapreneurs.com/2017/02/06/league-intrapreneurs-toolkit-sharing-lessons-field/

REFERENCES

Ahmed, Sayed Masud, et al. 'Bangladesh Health System Review'. Asia Pacific Observatory on Public Health Systems and Policies. *Health Systems in Transition,* Vol. 5, Issue 3, 2015.

Banerjee, Abhijit V., and Esther Duflo. 2011. *Poor Economics: A Radical Rethinking of the Way to Fight Global Poverty.* New York: PublicAffairs.

Blank, Steve. 'Part I: Validate Your Business Model Start with a Business Model, Not a Business Plan'. *Wall Street Journal,* 26 November 2012; http://blogs.wsj.com/accelerators/2012/11/26/start-with-a-business-model-not-a-business-plan/

Bugg-Levine, Antony, and Jed Emerson. 2011. *Impact Investing: Transforming How We Make Money While Making a Difference.* Hoboken: Jossey-Bass.

Croll, Alistair, and Ben Yoskovitz. 2013. *Lean Analytics: Use Data to Build a Better Startup Faster.* Sebastopol: O'Reilly.

Dees, J. Gregory. 'The Meaning of Social Entrepreneurship'. Stanford University. Last modified 30 May 2001; https://entrepreneurship.duke.edu/news-item/the-meaning-of-social-entrepreneurship/

Dees, J. Gregory. 'The Open Solutions Society'. Talk at PNCA, Portland, Oregon, 9 November 2012.

Ditkoff, Susan Wolf, et al. 2017. 'Onward: Accelerating the Impact of Social Impact Education'. Skoll Foundation. Accessed 12 May 2017; https://www.bridgespan.org/bridgespan/Images/articles/social-impact-education/Skoll_SocialImpactCenters-2017-04-18.pdf?ext=.pdf

Epstein, Marc J., and Kristi Yuthas. 2014. *Measuring and Improving Social Impacts: A Guide for Nonprofits, Companies, and Impact Investors*. San Francisco: Berrett-Koehler.

Fisher, Martin. 'Income Is Development'. *MIT Innovations*. Winter 2006.

Food and Agriculture Organization of the United Nations. 2019. 'Bangladesh'. FAOSTAT. Accessed 15 April 2019; http://www.fao.org/docrep/015/i2490e/i2490e01b.pdf

Food and Agriculture Organization of the United Nations. 2012. 'FAO Statistical Yearbook 2012'. Accessed 12 May 2017; http://www.fao.org/docrep/015/i2490e/i2490e01b.pdf

Foster, Malcolm. 'Cell Phones Vital in Developing World'. *The Associated Press*, 27 January 2007; http://www.washingtonpost.com/wp-dyn/content/article/2007/01/27/AR2007012700662_pf.html

Government of Bangladesh. 'Millennium Development Goals Bangladesh Progress Report 2015'. General

Economics Division (GED), Bangladesh Planning Commission, Government of the People's Republic of Bangladesh, 2015.

Grameenphone. 'About'. Accessed 14 August 2015; https://www.grameenphone.com/about

Grameen Communications. 'Grameen Bank Monthly Update in US$: August, 2014'. Last modified 7 September 2014; http://www.grameen-info.org/index.php?option=com_content&task=view&id=453&Itemid=527

Grameen Healthcare Trust. 'About'. Grameenhealth.org. Accessed 14 August 2015; http://grameenhealth.org/about.html

Grameen Kalyan. 'Health Care Programmes'. Grameen Kalyan. Accessed 28 June 2016; http://www.grameenkalyan-info.org/

Grameenphone. 'Company Profile'. Accessed 6 September 2016; https://www.grameenphone.com/about/investor-relations/

Grameen Shakti. 'Grameen Shakti'. Accessed 14 August 2015.

Gray, Jacob, et al. 2013. 'Great Expectations: Mission Preservation and Financial Performance in Impact Investing'. Wharton Social Impact Initiative. Last modified 2015; https://socialimpact.wharton.upenn.edu/wp-content/uploads/2016/09/Great-Expectations-Mission-Preservation-and-Financial-Performance-in-Impact-Investing.pdf

IFAD. 'Rural Poverty in Bangladesh'. Accessed 24 April 2017; https://www.ifad.org/en/web/operations/country/id/bangladesh

Intel Capital. 'Our Focus'. Accessed 6 July 2015; http://www.intelcapital.com/advantage/index.html

International Labour Organization. 'World Employment and Social Outlook: Trends 2016'. Accessed 12 May 2017; http://www.ilo.org/global/research/global-reports/weso/2016/WCMS_443480/lang--en/index.htm

Kaufmann, Daniel. 'Aid Effectiveness and Governance: The Good, the Bad and the Ugly'. *Brookings Institution*. Last modified 17 March 2009; http://www.brookings.edu/research/opinions/2009/03/17-aid-governance-kaufmann#figure

KickStart. 'Success Stories'. Accessed 24 April 2017; http://kickstart.org/impact/#success-stories

Kirsch, Walden. 'Women's Health Wearable for the Developing World'. *iQ.*, 11 August 2016. Internal Intel document.

Martinez, Michael. 'Red Cross Responds to Report about Building Only Six Homes in Haiti after 2010 Quake'. *CNN*, 4 June 2015; https://www.cnn.com/2015/06/04/americas/american-red-cross-haiti-controversy-propublica-npr/index.html

Mudaliar, Abhilash. '2016 Annual Impact Investor Survey'. Global Impact Investing Network. 18 May 2016; https://thegiin.org/knowledge/publication/annualsurvey2016

Murray, Christopher J.L., et al. 'Global, Regional, and National Incidence and Mortality for HIV, Tuberculosis, and Malaria during 1990–2013: A Systematic Analysis for the Global Burden of Disease Study 2013'. *Lancet*, 384(9947), 2014, pp. 1005–1070.

OLPC Foundation. 'Financial Statements'. 31 December 2007; http://wiki.laptop.org/images/e/ed/OLPCFAud-2007.pdf

Paulpolak.com. 'About Paul'. Accessed 24 April 2017; http://www.paulpolak.com/about-paul/

Pew Research Center. 'Remittance Flows Worldwide in 2017'. 3 April 2019; http://www.pewglobal.org/interactives/remittance-map/

Pinchot III, Gifford, and Elizabeth S. Pinchot. 'Intra-Corporate Entrepreneurship'. Intrapreneur. Last modified 1978; https://drive.google.com/file/d/0B6GgwqtG-DKcSlpsbGRBZkZYSlk/view

Polak, Paul. 'The Death of Appropriate Technology: If You Can't Sell It, Don't Do It'. Paulpolak.com. Last modified 10 September 2010; http://www.paulpolak.com/the-death-of-appropriate-technology-2/

Poushter, Jacob. 'Smartphone Ownership and Internet Usage Continues to Climb in Emerging Economies'. *Pew Research Center*. Last modified 22 February 2016; http://www.pewglobal.org/2016/02/22/smartphone-ownership-and-internet-usage-continues-to-climb-in-emerging-economies/

Prahalad, C.K., and Stuart L. Hart. 2008. 'The Fortune at the Bottom of the Pyramid'. *strategy+business* 26.

Quah, Danny. 'The World's Tightest Cluster of People'. *Global Policy Journal*. Last modified 26 April 2016; http://www.globalpolicyjournal.com/blog/26/04/2016/world%E2%80%99s-tightest-cluster-people

Ross, Brian, and Matthew Mosk. 'Fire Kills 112 Workers Making Clothes for US Brands'. *ABC*

News, 25 November 2012; https://abcnews.go.com/
Blotter/fire-kills-112-workers-making-clothes-us-
brands/story?id=17807229#.UX3ZKUpajX5

Shaffer, Richard. 'Unplanned Obsolescence'. *Fast Company,*
September 2007; https://www.fastcompany.com/
60302/unplanned-obsolescence

Starr, Kevin, and Laura Hattendorf. 'Real World Impact
Measurement'. *Stanford Social Innovation Review,*
24 September 2012; https://ssir.org/articles/entry/
real_world_impact_measurement

Tayabali, Rizwan. 2014. 'PATRI Framework for Scaling
Social Impact'. Ashoka Globalizer. Accessed 12 May
2017; https://issuu.com/ashokachangemakers/docs/
patri-framework

Thomas, Dana. 'Why Won't We Learn from the Survivors
of the Rana Plaza Disaster?' *New York Times,* 24
April 2018; https://www.nytimes.com/2018/04/24/
style/survivors-of-rana-plaza-disaster.html

'Towards the end of poverty'. *The Economist,* 1 June
2013.

'Trends in Social Innovation Education 2014'.
Washington DC: Ashoka U.

United Nations. 'The Millennium Development Goals
Report 2015'. Accessed 12 May 2017; http://
www.un.org/millenniumgoals/2015_MDG_Report/
pdf/MDG%202015%20rev%20(July%201).
pdf

United Nations. 2015. 'Transforming Our World: The
2030 Agenda for Sustainable Development'. Accessed
12 May 2017; http://www.un.org/ga/search/view_
doc.asp?symbol=A/RES/70/1&Lang=E

United Nations Millennium Project. 'About MDGs–What They Are'. Last modified 2006; https://www.un.org/millenniumgoals/

Vodafone. 2014. 'Mobilising Development'. Last modified 2016; https://www.vodafone.com/content/dam/sustainability/2015/pdf/vodafone-full-report-2015.pdf

World Bank. 'Bangladesh'. Accessed 24 April 2017; http://data.worldbank.org/country/bangladesh

World Bank. 2015. 'A Measured Approach to Ending Poverty and Boosting Shared Prosperity: Concepts, Data, and the Twin Goals'. doi:10.1596/978-1-4648-0361-1

World Food Programme of the United Nations. 2015. 'Who Are the Hungry?' Accessed 12 May 2017; https://www.wfp.org/hunger/who-are

World Health Organization. 'Bangladesh Statistics Summary'. Accessed 28 June 2016; http://apps.who.int/gho/data/node.country.country-BGD

World Health Organization. 'Household (Indoor) Air Pollution'. Accessed 8 November 2016; https://www.who.int/phe/air/en/

World Health Organization. 'Global Tuberculosis Report 2016'. Accessed 24 April 2017; https://apps.who.int/medicinedocs/documents/s23098en/s23098en.pdf

Yunus, Muhammad. 2010. *Building Social Business: The New Kind of Capitalism that Serves Humanity's Most Pressing Needs*. New York: PublicAffairs.

Yunus, Muhammad. 2008. *Creating a World Without Poverty: Social Business and the Future of Capitalism*. New York: PublicAffairs.

Zukin, Cliff, and Mark Szeltner. 'Talent Report: What
    Workers Want in 2012'. Net Impact. May 2012;
    https://netimpact.org/sites/default/files/documents/
    what-workers-want-2012.pdf

ACKNOWLEDGEMENTS

To my younger brother, Ehsan, who taught me anything is possible. To my father and mother, for fostering an interest in computers which opened a whole new world of opportunities. To my wonderful daughters, Alyssa and Alayna, for being blunt critics on the early version of the manuscript. To my wife, Nita, who balanced a career, children's school, sports, and a million other things during my travels. She was there every step of the way while still encouraging me to pursue more. To my father and mother in-law, for our discussions on international politics and world travel. To my extended family who has always believed in me and given me the confidence to aim big. Faruq, without whom I would not be able to navigate the city of Dhaka. On the professional front, Todd Underwood and Jeff Woolard, Intel executives, who were able to carve out some space for my risk-taking in the early years while simultaneously helping me balance my Intel priorities.— Kazi I. Huque

To my mother, Sharon, who taught me to write and to love writing. Thank you to Cindy Cooper, who started me on the path of social entrepreneurship and supported my work on this book, and to Crystal Greene, my wonderful wife and partner in all things.—Jacen Greene

To my Patti (grandmother), my guiding light. Thanks to my parents, who instilled in me the importance of giving back to society at all times and showed by example that there is a bigger purpose in life. To my wife Rani, who is the source of all my strength (and a lot of my ideas as well) and inspiration. Her patience and continuing support during the decade of constant travel to Asia, her listening sessions and thoughtful feedback on every aspect of my work are what keeps me going. To my two wonderful kids, Smaran and Dhyana, who constantly teach me to live every day with zest and enthusiasm as if everything is a miracle. To the Panneer Soda Gumbal, my crazy cousins and extended family who keep me honest and grounded, thank you. At Intel, all this would not have been possible without Lakshman Krishnamurthy, my manager, friend and confidante who supports me in following my passion and brings out the best in me through radical candour; and gratitude to Steve Holmes, for his unwavering support and belief that we should use cutting-edge technologies to help the underprivileged.— Narayan Sundararajan

Our experience shows how working across borders and different backgrounds can create a powerful new experience for the greater good. The following is a reflection of that.

Everything we talk about in our book, whether it's technology development or field work, would not have been possible without the Grameen Intel employees based in Bangladesh. On a daily basis they are not only faced with a strenuous commute and bandwidth challenges, but also put up with us wanting to do more and faster. Development work is never easy, but this book would not be possible without their grit and perseverance. Here are some of them: Pavel, Zia, Razib, Fakrul, Rashed, Arefeen, Fahim, Pritom, Nasrin, Firoz, Mamshad, Shahidul, Avizet, Nafis, Debashish, Tauhed, Sutapa, Anika, Jui, Laboni Nuzhat, Saqif, Sadman, Biswajit, Rehana, Tahsin, Isaba, Ziarot, Shariful, Maksud and many others who were with us on this exciting journey. To the support staff, Mintu, Zakir and Alif, without whose help the office would not function. To Srinivas in India and Dilek in Germany, our first business development managers who gave it all to bring in the first set of customers.

To our current and former board members, Professor Muhammad Yunus, Lamiya Morshed, Professor H.I. Latifee, Abdul Hai and John Davies, for being supportive and at the same time challenging us with many of our ideas.

Sincere thanks to the Intel team who all have their day jobs but volunteered with a lot of the product development and testing. For our COEL product, many thanks to Mourad, Shanmugam, Indulis, Braxton, Arjun, Kiran, Cindy, Alan, Isaac, Steve Ashok, Eiryanna and so many others. For the digital soil-testing kit, thanks to Tony, Imran, Leandro, Tara, Grace, Rod and many others behind the scenes. Thanks to Nithya and Martin from Nexleaf Analytics for multiple discussions and being wonderful collaborators sharing the same passion.

Thanks to the Penguin Random House team—Radhika, Bidisha, Khyati, Aakriti, Clare and others for their tireless efforts! To the entrepreneurs who want to make an impact, your only limitation is your own perseverance.